FOREWORD BY BARBARA J. YODER

NEW
BREED ARISING

Bridging the generations for strategic purpose

BENJAMIN ADAM DEITRICK

DEDICATION

This Book is dedicated to my wife who has believed in me from day one. She encouraged me to write, to dream and to believe that I could bring forth this vision from my heart. I love you Tarrah!

This book is also dedicated to Barbara J. Yoder who is the, "Samuel" in my life. Thank you for believing in me and pouring the oil of the Holy Spirit upon me time and again.

Finally, this book is dedicated to my children, Faith and Lily. May you walk in the purposes of God in your generation. May you encounter Jesus and know him for yourselves. Daddy loves you.

Acknowledgements

I want to acknowledge and thank everyone who wrote an endorsement for this book. Thank you for your kind words. Thank you also for your leadership in the Body of Christ.

I want to acknowledge and thank Hannah McKenley who poured over the original manuscript of this book and spent lots of hours correcting grammar, editing and working with me. Your work is very much appreciated.

Finally, I would like to acknowledge Kathryn R. Deering who did the final edit of this manuscript. Your expertise has made this a much better book. I am truly grateful.

CONTENTS

Introduction

Chapter 1: A Transitional Generation
Everything is Changing

Chapter 2: Decoding David
Understanding and Engaging the Younger Generations

Chapter 3: Saul or Samuel?
Don't Confuse a Saul with a Samuel...

Chapter 4: Understanding the Saul Structure
Unmasking this Ungodly Spirit

Chapter 5: Samuels, Arise!
Time for the Older Generation to Pour the Oil

Chapter 6: Kill Your Lion and Bear and *Then* We'll Talk...
Character Development for David

Chapter 7: The Call of Seduction
A Giant That Stands in Our Way...

Chapter 8: Hope Solutions
Encounter the Master of Breakthroughs

Chapter 9: David's Tent
An Apostolic People Who Rule

Chapter 10: Becoming the Bridge
In Times of Crisis, the Wise Build Bridges

ENDORSEMENTS FOR NEW BREED ARISING

In his timely book, *New Breed Arising*, Pastor Benjamin Deitrick releases powerful prophetic insight for the next generation of Kingdom leaders while encouraging and strengthening the previous generation. He manages to capture the heart of God for generational reform and revival. This is an on-target word much-needed for this time as we embark on a stunning journey of radical transformation and growth in the body of Christ. To go this distance, we must have teaching and revelation such as this book. This message will equip you for the challenges at hand and the time that is yet to come.

Ryan LeStrange
Author of Overcoming Spiritual Attack and Supernatural Access
Founder of TRIBE Network
Founder of Ryan LeStrange Ministries

I have known Benjamin for nearly twenty years now and I have had the privilege of watching him grow into the man he is today, a man full of integrity, honor and wisdom, a family man who loves God, his family and the Church. His passion for the existing generations to find a common ground with each other is so well presented in his book, *New Breed Arising*. Benjamin expresses God's heart in bringing the "heart of the fathers to the children, and the heart of the children to the fathers." This timely book will inspire all the generations to reach out to each other, with honor, respect and unity. Whether you are a Millennial, Boomer, GenX, whatever you may be, he offers wisdom to understand how each one thinks, and how we can glean from each other. As part of the generation before Benjamin, I am so filled with promise and hope of knowing that there are young men like him who deeply care about the future, past and present generations. This timely piece of God's mandate for the earth is a must read for all, young and old. We have so much to learn from each other and *New Breed Arising* is the perfect tool to help us understand, love and appreciate all the generations. You, too, will be motivated with new hope and promise when you read *New Breed Arising.*

Steve Swanson
Friends of the Bridegroom Worship Ministries

I love this book. It is a message from God's heart to His people. Yes, a new breed is rising and Holy Spirit will empower them to startle the world. Their passion and commitment to Christ will bring world-changing reform and expand His Kingdom. Holy Spirit has used Benjamin to write a vital and strategic word for our times. Read it prayerfully. Let the new breed arise. Let the generations surge together.

Apostle Tim Sheets
The Oasis Church, Middletown, Ohio
Tim Sheets Ministries
Awakening Now Prayer Network
Author of *Angel Armies, Planting the Heavens*, and other titles

Benjamin Deitrick's remarkable book *New Breed Arising* is a much-longed-for, much-needed resource for today's Church. I remember how quickened I was when he let me read some of his first pages as the book was being birthed. I thought, "Oh, this is going to be a good one!" And it is! Although it comes at a crucial time in the life of the Church today, I believe it will remain a timeless asset for years to come as we struggle to learn how to create a culture of honor that unites us all cross-generationally. The Davids will always need their Samuels; the Joshuas will always need their Moseses; the Elishas will always need their Elijahs. Benjamin's book is rich with transitional insights.

Mary Audrey Raycroft
Equipping Pastor, Catch the Fire, Toronto
Founder, Unbridled Ministries

This is a book for this generation. Benjamin does an outstanding job of presenting the needs of both the older and younger generations of saints. Benjamin gives a balanced and present truth presentation of how the generations can work together. The wisdom and anointing of the Samuels blended with the creativity and zeal of the Davids is going to bring about the greatest move of God in Church history. Thanks, Benjamin, for not just giving information and discussing the problem but also presenting creative ideas and revelation about how the generations can work in unity and demonstrate the Kingdom of God. This is a book you must read and assimilate if you want to unite the generations and activate them into being warriors in God's present-day army.

Bishop Bill Hamon
Founder and Bishop, Christian International Apostolic-Global Network
Author, *The Eternal Church, Prophets and Personal Prophecy, Prophets and the Prophetic Movement, Prophets, Pitfalls, and Principles, Apostles/Prophets and the Coming Moves of God, The Day of the Saints, Who Am I and Why Am I here, Prophetic Scriptures Yet to be Fulfilled (3rd Reformation), 70 Reasons for Speaking in Tongues, How Can These Things Be?* and *God's World War III*

New Breed Arising by Benjamin Deitrick is a voice crying out in today's wilderness, calling for a synergy of the generations and their combined strength and wisdom to become a critical catalyst for change. Let's pray that teamwork and communication, honor and humility, Samuel's Oil and David's Passion, all working together, will indeed transform the Orphaned Shepherd into a Ruling King. Bravo, Pastor Benjamin! The older generation is ready to run with you!

Bernardine Wormley Daniels
Founder, Soterios Ministries, Inc
Founder, Strength to Strength, LLC
Pastoral Council, Shekinah Church, Ann Arbor, Michigan

I believe that Benjamin Deitrick is on the cutting edge as it relates to how God is bringing the generations together for His purpose. My first thought in reading *New Breed Arising* was "Wow!" The revelation and material was incredible. I thought to myself, *This is the expression of one who is tapped into a Generations Anointing.* He understands the working of how the generations should receive and complement one another. Benjamin Deitrick is able to take the old and infuse it into the new while still carrying a fresh anointing. The revelations that God has given him compel both young and old to be open to receive the blessings that are carried by each generation. His teachings uniquely connect us to a powerful, Kingdom-purposed lifestyle. This is a buy-a-copy-for-every-leader book. It will bless them all.

Bishop William Murphy Jr.
Senior Pastor, New Mount Moriah International Church, Pontiac, Michigan
Bishop of Intercessory Prayer, Full Gospel Baptist Church Fellowship

I have known Benjamin Deitrick for over ten years. I was blessed to watch him as a young adult serving behind the scenes of different ministries, where he was a hard worker who was faithful before the Lord when no one was looking. Then God began to turn His face toward Benjamin with favor, promotion and destiny, and still, he served faithfully. I can think of no one better than Benjamin Deitrick to speak about the crisis in our generations. This book is full of insights for everyone on how to walk together to produce generational synergy. You will be convicted, enlightened and impacted to walk out the pages of this book.

Julie Meyer
Apostolic Healing Rooms of Santa Maria Valley

FOREWORD

By: Barbara J. Yoder

Immersed in books, I'm desperately attempting to discover information that will connect my past spiritual journey with the future. I'm sitting in the middle of piles of books, some outstanding, some mediocre and most just a waste of time. There has to be something or someone who can inform my ignorance. I don't want to be in the dark, I want to be in the know. I'm aware of the fact that we've never lived in such a time of escalating change so I'm desperately searching for bridges to the future.

What I've just written sounds like a merry-go-round of confusion. In one sense it's because that's where we find ourselves, as we come out of confusion and find our footing for what is happening in the Church today. Emerging out of difficulty or devastation or even irrelevancy, the restored church is on track to becoming a society-transforming powerhouse (Isaiah 61).

I am part of the older generation. I know what has worked in the past, what we have believed and where we need to be going. Living close to Detroit has been an education in understanding societal change and the importance of the generations. Detroit used to be the fourth largest city in America. It was also the wealthiest city per capita in the United States from the 1940s through about 1965. But because of the racial riots in 1967 and the long tenure of Coleman Young as mayor starting in 1973, the automobile capital of America became a graveyard city. The middle class fled the city because of fear and corruption. The national recession of 2007 through 2008 brought Detroit to its knees. It plummeted to the bottom financially and in 2013 entered into bankruptcy. Yet now it's being called the comeback city.

What happened? One thing that has been extremely significant is that the younger generation moved in. They bought apartments and moved into the newly renovated lofts; they flooded the inner city along the river. Why? They saw the potential in Detroit. They saw the entrepreneurial void and realized that they carried the ideas that could change the future. Others saw it as a place where they could build their company for much less than in any other city. The city had hit rock bottom financially, so it was seeking to find those who could rebuild it financially. A couple of extremely wealthy and successful business owners moved their companies into downtown Detroit. Others like them helped fill the void. Mike Ilitch, now deceased, was the owner of Little Caesar's Pizza and a couple of the professional sports teams in Detroit. He was one of the key leaders who maintained vision for the city. He was perhaps the key player from the older generation. Now Detroit is on the verge of being restored as a thriving city. Two years ago it was voted as one of the top ten cities to visit on a weekend.

However, a significant fact is that most of the older generation who knew Detroit as it was in its glory days can only mourn the past. They cannot see the future. They need a bridge to help them move from the Detroit of the past to what Detroit is now. By themselves they cannot get there. Yet they carry wisdom, experience and knowledge beyond that of the younger generation. Furthermore, their anointing, the glory they carry, is way beyond almost all of the younger generation. They are like Samuel mourning Saul. God admonished Samuel to quit mourning Saul. It's similar to the way some of Israel's people responded to the rebuilding of the second Temple.

Benjamin Deitrick has written a book which embodies these truths. The church is at a crossroads. The church of the past is now in many ways outdated and powerless. To find our way to the future we need a new vision.

A friend of mine had a dream and I often refer to it when speaking. The dream was about the sinking of the Titanic, that most elegant and amazingly engineered luxury ocean liner that sank on its maiden voyage. I heard God say that, similar to its sinking, the church ministry machine of the past era has sunk. God is up to something new (see Isaiah 43:19–21).

I've seen amazing miraculous moves of God. Yet for a while it has seemed as though we are in a lull. There are good, even great, things happening spiritually, yet something feels absent. I believe Benjamin has his finger on the pulse of the new thing that God is doing. There is a new generation arising that spans the ages, from young to old. From this "new generation" a company of reformers will arise to greatly change the face of the church. We've heard again and again since the early 90s that the church is not going to look the same in the future. Some prophets have even said that we won't recognize it. To be honest, for the most part, it still looks the same to me. So we are still looking toward the future.

The bottom line to all of this is that we can't do it alone. Moses needed Joshua and vice versa. Elisha and Elijah needed each other. Timothy needed Paul. Paul needed a Timothy to reproduce himself in, someone to carry his heart and vision. Ruth created a fresh lineage for Naomi that became a precursor to the Messiah, "the new thing." Abraham, Isaac and Jacob each added another piece to the puzzle, a three-generation powerhouse.

This new generation is arising, comprised of multiple generations who are being formed into a formidable, powerful, redemptive, God-loving people. They are the loving, honoring, miracle-working and reforming *new breed*. They have emerged from a worn-out manmade mold to create the new Church, founded on the Word and birthed by the Spirit.

Barbara J Yoder
Lead Apostle, Speaker and Author
Shekinah Regional Apostolic Center
Ann Arbor, Michigan

INTRODUCTION

She accepted the expertly folded American flag with trembling hands as she said goodbye to the other half of her heart. The flag was being given out of honor for a soldier who had fought bravely in World War II against an unspeakable evil. As she looked upon the casket her eyes began to fill with tears. Suddenly she couldn't contain it anymore. She fell upon the wooden structure that had become her husband's final place of rest. Her shrill cry rang out and pierced my ears and my heart like an arrow. She wept as the honor guard began to play a marching rhythm that began to drown out all other sounds.

Truth be told, it was one of the first funerals I had ever been to. I was not personally tied to the loved one who had passed away and was in attendance only out of respect for a friend. But something filled me as that woman, newly widowed, began to cry—a sudden rush of knowledge that the generation this man represented was quickly leaving the earth. His friends who surrounded the casket looked frail and weak. I suddenly felt very sad, as if something very valuable was leaving, never to return.

As I rode home from the ceremony with a friend, eyes welling with tears, he could tell I was feeling something very deeply. He asked me what was wrong and my answer was simple: "What that old man represented is not present in my generation . . . and we need it now more than ever."

You see, I was not raised in a time where you could leave your doors unlocked at night and trust that all would be well. My friends and I did not run all around town with liberty, instinctively knowing that we should be back at sundown. Instead, I was raised in a time when people would lock and deadbolt their doors, set their alarms and even then stay up at night at times wondering what could happen. Times have changed, and they have changed faster and more dramatically in the past hundred years than I think anyone could have possibly imagined.

Institutions of family, religion, law and government, although never perfect, have been eroding over the years at a rate that at times seems almost irreparable. As I write this in the year 2016, there seems to be no clear moral compass whatsoever as we look around desperately for leaders to guide us. Those who should be in what is referred to as the "sage" stage of life are often disregarded as irrelevant as we race forward into "progress."

There is more knowledge now available at the tip of a finger than ever before, but where is the true wisdom? Where are the elders in our time to help to guide and shape the next generation? And does the next generation even want what they could offer? We have come to a moment of crisis.

There is an old Nigerian saying: "In the moment of crisis, the wise build bridges and the foolish build dams." The truth of this statement has profoundly impacted my life in the past several years.

What bridges do we need? When I look at those bridges that need to be built, one of the most important is the bridge between the generations. Bridges bring unity and we need unity. We need a unity that is not only manifested in words of honor toward one another, but a unity that is functional; a unity that works. There is so much to be accomplished in this important time and it will not happen unless young and old work together.

In this book, my goal is to incite a revolution. I want to shake our generations out of their status quo and to help guide us to where we need to be. I want to awaken us to the unique purpose of each generation and to provide hope, vision, and practical steps to journey down the path together.

In this book I will be speaking primarily to two groups of people: the older generation and the younger generation. You can find yourself in one of those categories and choose which one you feel you identify with (and I am aware there are many who will probably feel caught in between). The premise of this book is taken out of the interwoven lives of three main characters in the Bible: Samuel, Saul and David. I am going to be looking at the older generation as Samuels and Sauls and the younger generation as Davids.

We have come to a moment where all over the world whether in business, economics, technology, fashion or religion, a younger generation has not only come of age, but are in positions of great responsibility and leadership. They are a force to be reckoned with, and have accomplished great things in their short time on the scene, but have also been met with a lot of misunderstanding and frustration. They don't fit anyone's mold and in fact that is the farthest thing from their minds. They want to do things their way and they really don't think they need any help from anyone.

All the while the older generation in some cases is handing over the baton to these people who are young enough to be their children and grandchildren and doing so with not a little bit of trepidation. They wonder in many cases what is to become of what they have built on their blood, sweat and tears. Their generation worked hard and sacrificed, but they feel this generation knows nothing of the sort. Many see the younger generations as lazy, undisciplined, arrogant and naïve.

There have been countless articles, documentaries and studies done on this subject. I am not an expert in those nor have I tried to become so in this midst of this project. My heart is to point out the "God opportunity" in the midst of this unique scenario. There is a plan and purpose in the heart of God in all of this that will bring about a synergy of the generations, which will in turn usher in a massive move of God. This will happen because Saul's kingdom is crumbling, Samuel is full of oil and David is ready to be anointed. The orphan shepherd will be transformed into a ruling king—one after God's own heart. The arrogance of his heart will fade away in the lessons that come with the anointing and the Glory will come in the tent he sets up for God. And God will rule and reign from that place of Presence. Let's journey together into this process and witness the transformation.

Chapter 1

A TRANSITIONAL GENERATION

Everything is Changing

We are living in a very important time in the Body of Christ. In many ways, it is a transitional place for us all. We are shifting out of a traditional organizational culture to one that captures the heart of chapter 2 of the book of Acts again. There is a cry in the hearts of the people for the real, raw and authentic. Revival is breaking out all around the world in Asia, Africa, South America and in hundreds of hidden places no one even knows about. Training, equipping and revival centers are springing up all over the place and there is a huge change in the way that many are "doing church." The rigidity of the way that we have structured things in the past isn't working anymore and many are awakening to the realization that a massive change is upon us. I believe, as many do, that this restructuring is needed because of a great harvest that is about to come. There is a tsunami wave of fire beginning to crash upon the shores of all the earth and spreading with a torrential force. Many have prophesied that another billion souls are coming into the kingdom. It is as if the global Church has stepped into a new era. Something huge is happening.

What will this shift bring? How should this next wave be led and guided? I personally feel that if we are to see the fullness of this next move come forth that there has to be a working together and a synergy of the generations as never before. We live in a unique time where there are several generations alive on the earth together. This is somewhat of an anomaly when you look at the past 500 years. Life expectancy has jumped dramatically in the past one hundred years and this has created an environment of unique possibility. No longer are we losing the older generation prematurely. We now have much more time to receive their wisdom, counsel and experience. God is the God of Abraham, Isaac and Jacob! He has a plan, part and purpose for all the generations to fulfill. It is imperative in this time that we come together in a unity that is functional and will move us forward in effective intergenerational leadership. This great harvest is going to take all of us, each doing our part. No one generation can do it alone.

As 1 Corinthians 16:9 puts it, a great and effective door has opened up to us. We have to step over the threshold together. The threshold is the place of transition, but it is also a treacherous and fragile place. We need great wisdom to know how to move across it. The nation of Israel came to a very important moment of transition in the time of Samuel when God was removing the leadership of Saul and installing David as the new king. David had been anointed. The prophet had come, the oil had been poured and the mantle had fallen on David. God had clearly said that he had removed the kingdom from the house of Saul and his descendants and had given it to the house of David. However, David still had to war with the house of Saul and hang out in caves while Saul was in the palace; there was war between the house and Saul and the house of David for many years (see 2 Samuel 3:1).

He had the anointing, but not the position. They were in a transitional time. Something was happening, but it had not yet come to pass.

This so clearly mirrors much of what is happening in the Body of Christ right now. There is a clear shift from the house or rule of Saul to the heart and rule of David. The structure of Saul is a structure that has been appointed by man to serve man. It holds onto a religious system in an effort to maintain power and control. The heart of David serves the Lord. This is the anointing that Mike Bickel, Lou Engle, Dutch Sheets and so many others have been trumpeting for years now—a heart for "one thing" (see Psalm 27:4). The heart of David cares little for religious tradition and structure, but desires the presence of God more than anything. We are in the time when God is restoring the Tabernacle of David as he promised in the book of Amos (see Amos 9:11). This restoration comes through an apostolic anointing that issues forth the government of God across entire nations. God has been preparing a generation and is getting ready to launch them on a large scale with this Davidic anointing to rule. I believe that the young people who are alive today are called as a David generation. This David generation is a unique and multi-gifted group, bursting with potential.

I want to pause here to honor the Reverend Dr. Robert Stearns who was the first to introduce me to these concepts. His insights into these matters were revolutionary to me when I was just starting in ministry. I have since preached messages and have heard others expound on these ideas, but all of the messages have focused for the most part on the two main players; David and Saul. In this first chapter, however, I want to point our attention to another player who has not been mentioned in the dialogue as much: Samuel.

I feel that Samuel represents the older generations alive on the earth right now. Some in these generations are retired and some of them are not in good health; however, in this season God is going to be renewing their strength in an amazing way. When I have talked them, some have even wondered what the Lord could or would possibly use them for in this time. I want to say clearly that these generations have yet to play an extremely important role in the whole unfolding of this transitional time and in the passing of the mantle to David. In fact, in many ways, prophetically, they are the key to opening wide this door of harvest and revival. For many in this generation reading this, your best days are yet ahead of you!

As we delve into this, allow me to clarify something. I have often heard the statement that the "older generation" is a "Saul" and that God is constantly raising up a new generation of Davids who will break people out of tradition, etc. A blanket statement like this is a fallacy. It seems to imply that if you are old, you are a Saul, and if you are young, you are a David. Many who have said this have confused order with control and said this out of a wounding and distrust.

God is a God of honor and respect and even holy order. Just because someone is older and sets things in order at times does not mean they are a "Saul." Saul was in fact forty years older than David and in a sense was a father figure in his life as his literal father-in-law. David served in the house of Saul for seven years somewhere around the time after his victory over Goliath. David was also close friends with Saul's son Jonathan, which could imply a certain level of closeness or relationship between the two. However, these facts do not translate into blanket statements about age or generation as we draw a correlation between the house of Saul and the house of David.

Anyone of any age can be operating out of a Saul system, and anyone of any age can be like a David. Just because I feel specifically that the younger generations have a David calling does not mean that this anointing is limited to them. I am simply drawing parallels which will speak to the potential and destiny within each generation.

Don't Confuse a Samuel with a Saul

The other challenge and pitfall of painting the older generation with this generalization is that many will miss their Samuel because they will confuse him with a Saul. Just because they are both older does not mean that they represent the same things.

We have to remember from where the anointing came onto David. It was from Samuel! It was not from Jesse, David's father, or from Obed, his grandfather. It was not from the deflated King Saul after he failed. It was not from the people of the nation of Israel. The anointing came to David from the prophet of God, who had the mantle to lead.

Many times people see Samuel as "just a prophet" who spoke the word of the Lord. Sometimes as a child when I would read about Samuel I would get some pretty funny mental pictures. (Picture an old man living alone on a mountain, descending to say a few words and then disappearing again, a strange person with limited social interaction and tattered clothes who ate strange foods, and so forth. My brother and I would sometimes make up stories and joke with one another about the prophets in the Bible and what they were like.)

But whatever Samuel actually looked like or how he acted, we need to remember that Samuel was truly the legitimate voice of leadership to the entire nation of Israel. Like many other prophets and judges of Israel before him, from Moses forward, he was not a marginalized and truncated voice to the nation who was heeded sometimes and other times not. No, Samuel was the final authority on matters concerning the direction of the nation. The Bible says that God *"let none of his words fall to the ground"* (1 Samuel 3:19, NKJV).

Therefore, because he *had* the legitimate mantle to lead, he was able to *give* and *impart* the mantle to lead!

This is why we need to respect and look to the Samuels in our generation; they are the ones who are anointed and actually have the authority to set up and empower leadership. Even if Saul had wanted to anoint and empower David to lead in his stead, he could not have. *He had the position, but he didn't have the authority.*

The younger generations need eyes to see and true discernment in this matter so that they will not allow the blindness that comes from wounding to hinder their relationships. You see, the younger generations greatly distrust the older generations. I am going to expound on that more in the chapters to come, because this is a serious hindrance and stumbling block that is affecting many and causing division where God wants to bring unity.

The younger generations have been let down by institutions. Statistically speaking, every institution that was supposed to support, guide and undergird them has let them down over and again. The marriage institution, the Church with all of the sex scandals and financial schemes, the breakdown of the sense of community and safety in the environments they grew up in, and on and on. This wounding has gone deep. Even though it is not unjustifiable, it is causing blindness to the younger generations, who have so much to learn from the older generations, but who many times shy away from what they have to offer because of this woundedness.

Samuel Is Looking for a David to Anoint

There is a whole generation of Samuels in leadership right now in the Body of Christ that I have the utmost respect for. Two people I want to honor who are Samuels in my life are Apostle Barbara J. Yoder and Mary Audrey Raycroft. Apostle Barbara J. Yoder is the founder of the Apostolic Center I lead in Ann Arbor, Michigan. Mary Audrey Raycroft is a close family friend and was the equipping pastor for Catch the Fire in Toronto, Ontario. Her ministry was used mightily in the breaking out of revival that swept over that place and spread across the world. God has used these two women over and again as voices of reason, wisdom and spiritual awakening in my life. I honestly don't know where I would be without them. I can think of others, too, such as Bishop Bill Hamon and Mahesh and Bonnie Chavda. Also Derek Prince, C. Peter Wagner and many more who have gone on to be with the Lord. I think of all that they have done for the Body of Christ. The quality of leadership in their generation has not been matched, in my opinion, when you consider the implications of what they have built and put in place.

This generation of leaders has paid the price to do what is right over and again and they have maintained the utmost integrity in everything. They have built solidly, led well, and have had a major impact, bringing millions of people into the kingdom of God. In addition, they have spearheaded the move of God and have helped to lead and guide the Body of Christ to this place of transition where we are now.

They have done all of this, yet most of them are aware of one very poignant reality: They cannot do this forever. Where and to whom can they look? When they appraise the generations coming after them, they have some serious concerns, and they wonder what will happen in the future. They are looking for a David whom they can anoint and empower.

Some of these great leaders have put others in place to take up their mantle just as Samuel did in Scripture. We read in 1 Samuel 8 that Samuel had appointed his sons to rule in his place, but it had not gone well. *"But his sons did not walk in his ways; they turned aside after dishonest gain, took bribes, and perverted justice"* (1 Samuel 8:3, NKJV). This failure of Samuel's sons was ultimately what led to the people of Israel to ask for a king. The implications of that were far-reaching and in many ways they took Israel away from God's original intent.

Look at the structure of Israel before Saul came onto the scene—really it was led in a theocratic way. Prophets and judges heard from God and guided the people of Israel. There was succession from one prophet or judge to another. They had never had a king; they had never needed a king. But when Samuel's sons did not walk in the ways of the Lord and failed in their leadership, there was no prophetic succession.

Many of the leaders of the older generation have lived through a failed succession and have seen the effects and results. Many have been greatly harmed by these failures. Therefore, as they look out over the landscape of the future, they do not want to make the same mistake. It is too easy to misinterpret this reluctance as not wanting to move out of the way or give up control. People say to them, "It's time to move over and let youth lead."

This puts the older generation in a spot, to be honest. Many of the people that these Samuel leaders are trying to pass their mantle to are younger people, men and women in their early thirties or forties. They may have looked like Davids, but they really weren't. Just because someone is young and gifted doesn't mean that he or she is a David. We have to be so careful in judging by age or outward appearance and making generalizations.

What we need to realize is that it is not youth that leads, it is the anointing of the Lord and his mantle. If the anointing is not there, there can be no effective succession of leadership. In fact, with David, not only was he anointed by God, it was the entire process he went through that tested him and crushed him over and again that made him qualified and ready to lead. I will expound on that further as this book unfolds.

And so as leaders, these "Samuels" find that they are at a very critical juncture. They need the mind and wisdom of the Lord to know who to anoint for the future. To whom should they give their mantle? They need to choose wisely. The Samuels need to be working together with the Davids in this transitional season. Even though we do not see a lot of interaction between David and Samuel in the Bible, we ourselves need to work together if we are ever to see today's Davids begin to fulfill their purpose and calling.

Now you may be reading this and be forty-seven years old and not feel like a David at all. You may feel like a Samuel because of what the Lord has taken you through and done in your life. That is fine! Or you may be that same age and feel as though you bear the heart and passion of a David, because you can relate to the examples put forth in the previous section. That is also fine! I want to say to all who are reading this: Find yourself in the story. I am trying to use broad brushstrokes as much as I can in painting a picture of "older generations" and "younger generations." I am not trying to build cages for people to fit into, but rather to stir up a revolution where the old and young begin to work together.

You also may be a woman, young or old, and think to yourself, *I don't relate to all these male examples.* I can certainly understand that, but I personally believe that the examples and heroes of faith that God outlines for us in Scripture are not meant to be gender restrictive. For example, even as a man I know I am called to the kingdom for "such a time as this" (see Esther 4:14) and I draw strength and inspiration from the courage of Queen Esther. Likewise, those younger or older ladies reading this can find strength and inspiration from the authority and leadership of Samuel and the giant-slaying bravery of David. Again, as you read, just find yourself in the story and be encouraged to act and build and lead as God has called you to do!

In the next chapter, let's look together at beginning to figure out some of these "Davids in the field." There are some challenges along the way that Samuel leaders need to be aware of in looking for and then working with a real David.

Chapter 2

DECODING DAVID

Understanding and Engaging the Younger Generations

Language is such a powerful thing. It is the basis of intelligent communication and even surpasses the medium of words. You can communicate the language of your thoughts through your eyes, your body language, movements, gestures and so much more. Language connects us and causes us to be able to enter into the context of each other's thinking and feeling.

A man named Ludwig Wittgenstein once said, "The limits of my language are the limits of my world." What a powerful quote that is, especially when you consider what we are delving into in this book. If the generations are going to work together, we will have to speak each other's language, not only the language of the intellect, but the language of the heart. We will have to learn to decode those things that at times seem so confusing and bewildering. We will have to build bridges of unity and cooperation across the suspicion and fear that threatens to divide us and dig trenches between us.

How do we begin to decode each other, to peer into each other's worlds? I believe we begin by understanding. To understand, you first have to know. I have been asking myself the question a lot, "How much do I really know about the older generation?" How often have I stopped and asked questions before making assumptions? I believe there is a lot we need to know about each other before we are able to work together.

Let's look for a moment into the heart and mind of this David generation and perhaps come to know and understand a bit more about them, and where we might find them.

David Is in the Field

It is completely natural to follow the normal order of things. If you look at a river, it flows perfectly downstream and stays mostly within its banks and borders. Waterfalls flow from the top down in a beautiful display of power and grandeur. I have never looked outside and seen the rain coming from the ground up into the sky! There is an order of things, although sometimes in the kingdom of God, it's different, when he goes against the grain and paints outside the lines.

As the search for David begins, the natural thing to do is to look at the normal, created order of things. Samuel got a word from the Lord that among the sons of Jesse was the next king of Israel (see 1 Samuel 16:1). So he did the logical thing that any of us would have done and went to the house of Jesse. But *David wasn't in the house.*

In many ways today, I feel the house that Samuel went to look in is the church. We are thinking about raising up the next generation of leaders, so many times we do the natural, normal thing—we start to look in the church. Now, please hear me, there is nothing wrong with this. Raising up sons and daughters from within the house is admirable, right and good. But I feel in my heart that there is a whole new breed that is being raised up in this time. They aren't going to be where we expect them to be; in fact, they will be out of place. There is a harvest field out there that is white, just waiting for someone to have eyes to *see the potential and purpose in a few lowly shepherds who weren't even called to the table for the grand selection.*

Not only are many of these Davids not going to be where they are "supposed" to be, but they are not going to look or act the "normal" way that is expected, either.

Why am I saying this? In order for God to accomplish what he desires in this time, it is going to take a people who are willing to

26

be radical, who can operate outside the box. I just mentioned a few sentences ago that God paints outside the lines, many times. Who is willing to paint with him? There are masterpieces waiting to be created! God is challenging the established order, not to frustrate or to harm, but in order to create a structure that can handle the harvest with wisdom.

God does not pour new wine into old wineskins! God doesn't want any of this new wine to be wasted or spilled out on the ground. God is challenging the order of Saul that is built by, maintained by and ultimately serves the will and desire of man. He is looking for those Davids who don't have a religious bone in their bodies and who are willing to be radical and go against the grain in order to see God's heart and purpose established. What God is doing is so far out of our understanding and paradigm that if we love the structure of Saul, (the way things are currently) we will never be able to move into his new way.

God wants to harvest these radicals—those on the streets or in the drug houses; the gangbangers and prostitutes; the lonely, empty executives; the fashion designers; the intellectuals. He wants the down and out, the successful, the bored—a whole new generation of revivalists who will be captured by his call.

Now, don't get me wrong, some Davids are in the church. But the vast majority of them *need to be harvested.* This company of Davids is in the field, waiting to be called forth. That's why the Samuels in the Body of Christ need eyes to see what truly lies within each one. The Samuels need to look past the handsome, tall, *reasonable choice* in order to see the *unreasonable,* forgotten and neglected shepherd who bears the heart of God . . . and might not even be aware of it. All they need is an opportunity and an invitation.

Too often we see challenging the status quo and risking as negative things. But I believe that in the kingdom, risk is celebrated far more than safety. When did safety ever change the world? Only that which challenges the status quo has ever changed the world. In fact, the world and most people are programed to do what they have always done. But, if we want to see something happen that has never been done before, then we have got to be willing to do what has never been done before.

We need to begin to build a culture of risk rather than a culture of safety. In many ways the entire structure of the past season in the Church was built upon maintaining what we have attained. Maintain the big crowd, the big building and the big bucks and man, you're successful!

Not so! David is in the field. He may be nowhere near our big bucks and big buildings.

God is looking for a group of Samuels who are willing to take a risk on some pretty out-of-the-box, radical Davids to whom no one else would even give a chance. Can you see the treasure in the jars of clay? It's looking right back at you when you drive down the street or through a part of the neighborhood that you wouldn't normally venture into. David is waiting. Who will give him the opportunity and extend the invitation to divine purpose?

David Is an Orphan

Another important point the Samuels need to understand is that the Davids come from a totally different world than they do. The Davids do not come from a world of leaving the doors unlocked and running around with friends until dark. They weren't born into Samuel's America and they will never know it. The world they were born into is a war zone, by and large. Many in the younger generation, whether inside or outside the church, feel very lost.

There is speculation on this fact, but many theologians believe that David may have been an illegitimate child. Why wasn't he called in for the selection? Why was he tending the sheep alone? Why did he seem to always be in the service of his older brothers? He was the youngest and there certainly may have been some cultural realities that contributed to this, but there may have been something more here than meets the eye or the basic reading of the

Scripture. This thought is even alluded to in David's own writing in Psalm 51:5 when he says *"in sin my mother conceived me."*

Whatever the case was with the David of the Bible, I can say with certainty that one of the main things that today's younger generation struggles with is this feeling of being an orphan. Some would refer to it as the orphan spirit. I would refer to it as an orphan mindset or mentality.

This mindset is a formidable challenge for someone who struggles with it, and it colors his or her perception of all of life's events. When something happens, or doesn't happen, or happens a certain way, the thoughts are always the same; I'm alone, unwanted, rejected and insignificant. That feeling then leads to anger and all kinds of outworking of frustration. Their heart's cry is to be good enough, to matter, to be significant.

Some of the Davids that are in the field are struggling with all sorts of sins, having been driven into lifestyle choices by this mindset. If you do not think your life has any worth or value, no hope and no potential, you slip away into despair. People tend to live up (or down) to their own as well as others' expectations for their lives.

The other thing that this mindset creates is a sense of mistrust. The orphan expects to be let down, abandoned and abused. Many Samuels become frustrated with a David because it can be so difficult to connect in a real, authentic and vulnerable way. That is the orphan mindset at work. It refuses and is in fact incapable of trusting. There is no foundation of love and acceptance that would make that trust connection possible. Healing must take place.

Prophetically speaking, I believe that the Samuel generation carries an anointing that is going to bring massive healing to this issue. The Samuels have an oil to pour out that will bring about transformation.

Samuel anointed David and poured the horn of oil onto him:

Then Samuel took the horn of oil and anointed him in the midst of his brothers; and the Spirit of the LORD came upon David from that day forward. So Samuel arose and went to Ramah. (1 Samuel 16:13, NKJV)

Many times oil speaks of healing. Jeremiah 8:22 speaks of a balm of Gilead, an oil of healing. In Luke 10:34, Jesus makes reference to a Good Samaritan pouring on the soothing oil and the wine.

Oil also speaks of authority and appointing. It speaks of identity. I believe that as Samuel poured that horn of oil onto David, that there was an infusion of identity and purpose that brought healing to the orphan heart of David. This Samuel generation needs to know how much power they have resident in them and they need to begin to tip the horn of oil onto the orphans who are lost in the field.

I want to speak for a moment to grandparents. I have been speaking mainly in this section to the leaders in the Body of Christ who are like Samuels, with the authority to lead. But I want to say to this Samuel generation, that you are powerful whether you have a title and position or not. Your generation has seen things that the younger generation longs to see. You have lived through the healing revivals of the 1950s and the Jesus people movement of the 1970s. You saw and experienced the Toronto and Brownsville outpourings that happened when the younger generations were only teenagers or little children.

You have a depth of the knowledge of God that holds within it transformative power. Your grandchildren especially need you. They need your wisdom, your insight, your understanding and your love. The power rests within you to turn orphan shepherds into mighty kings who will lead in the days to come. Please do not be silent and do not underestimate the anointing within you. It is precious oil that is desperately needed.

There is a deliverance mantle falling onto you right now even as you read this. Put out your hands in front of you and ask the Lord to begin to impart a fresh anointing to you. Ask him to activate what is on the inside of you. Ask him to give you names and faces and words of knowledge of people you are called to speak to and meet. You are called to set these Davids free! I want to encourage you to start to reach out to the young people in your life, whomever they may be. They may have told you not to call them or they may have acted bored when you were with them, but try to see behind the lies.

One grandparent I know recently told me that her grandchild was greatly touched by her small acts of love. The grandmother never knew until years later that her calls and texts and little messages that were never responded to meant so much to the grandchild. They were seeds of love and they have yielded a harvest of relationship and intimacy in the years that have followed. Sometimes it is the simple, seemingly insignificant acts of love, kindness and affection that can make all the difference in someone's life.

Sometimes we make things so complicated. Some of the most powerful things you can do are as small as little mustard seeds at first, but they will grow large in the garden of someone's heart. You don't need to be overly religious or spiritual. You don't need to have nineteen verses that you employ in your strategy. You don't need to yell at demons in your young people on a church prayer line to have an impact. All you need to do is pick up the phone and invite a young person to lunch or for coffee. Listen, respond and love in the smallest ways and watch the transformation happen. Watch the royalty start to emerge in the life of your young person.

Apostle Barbara Yoder was preaching a message a few years ago. She was talking about the impact we have on people's lives and how we never really know who is sitting or standing before us. All of a sudden, she asked the question, "Who was Billy Graham's Sunday school teacher?"

That question pierced through me like an arrow. Who are the people we pass by everyday who have unlocked and untapped potential? What mighty man or woman of God do we pass over when we ignore a hyper little kid running circles around us? They just might be the next Billy Graham.

Never underestimate the impact your small acts can have on someone. Samuels, you are not insignificant or unneeded. You are vital to the emergence of this next move of God. The Davids cannot fulfill their call without you. Our destinies are more tied together than we realize.

Chapter 3

SAUL OR SAMUEL?

Don't Confuse a Saul with a Samuel...

The Bible says, *"Gray hair is a crown of splendor; it is attained in the way of righteousness"* (Proverbs 16:31, NIV). Someone once told me, "When you start to see the gray hairs dishonored, know that trouble is not far away." I have never forgotten that.

Growing up, I was raised as a Christian in a Mennonite home. The church was very small and led by a kind man who had a pastor's heart as well as a heart for the lost. He was always thinking up new ways to engage the community and honor those that were often forgotten.

My family has a long standing history with that church, in fact, over thirty years later, my parents still attend it. If you are a faithful church attender, you have probably heard someone say at some point, "I helped build this church with my own sweat, blood and tears!" In some cases, such a statement may be true in a figurative sense, but for my father, a statement like that is true in a very literal sense, because he helped to pour the very concrete of the foundation and put in countless hours of free labor. He wanted to help see a vision of a small church in a little-known community in Pennsylvania become a reality.

My brother, sister and I were always—and I mean, *always*—at church as children. Anything that was happening, we were there whether we wanted to be or not. On top of that, we were homeschooled. Are you beginning to get the picture? Our youth group was small, to say the least, and when we did have youth group it was often just my family and a few others. No black lights in the youth room with the cool couches set off to the side in the church building for us. I remember feeling almost scandalous as a twelve-year-old attending a Newsboys concert in the 1990s!

My mom was a stay-at-home mom while my dad worked very hard all his life with his hands, so the schooling was mostly left up to her. She was exceptionally intelligent, but there were many times that she needed to find something for us to do to round out one or another subject in our log books, as they were called. One of these activities was a weekly gathering at our church called Care and Share.

Sounds thrilling, I know, and believe me, it was. There were all kinds of things for this active boy who was nicknamed the Energizer Bunny (mostly because I ran up and down the stairs just for fun) to do, like knit, do puzzles and *sit and talk.* I loathed sitting and talking. It was like being put in prison. Didn't Mom know about the adventures that awaited me out of doors? But it didn't matter—I was sentenced to the Care and Share group for good. Little did I know how much *good* it would instill in me, nor did I know about the Samuel who was there waiting to have an impact on me.

You see, in case you hadn't guessed, this group was for senior citizens, people who had largely been forgotten by those around them. Many lived alone or with a single family member and although it felt to me like doing hard time to come to Care and Share, for many of these men and women, it was the highlight of their week. On one of the first weeks as I was sitting with one of the members of the group, enduring hearing about various health ailments again trying my best to be polite, a cheery British voice popped up behind me and said, "You there! Be a good lad and help me out." I didn't know who it was and I didn't care who it was or what needed to be done—I was in! I excused myself from the table and turned around to join my rescuer. I was met by a short, strong-looking older man with a good red color in his cheeks and a smile in his bright eyes.

34

Ron and his wife Audrey were new to the church, which is why I didn't recognize the voice speaking to me at first, but as soon as I turned around, I knew I was in for some fun. Ron and Audrey actually led this community group and I think that somehow Ron knew what kind of a time it was for me. He never looked down on me with a scowl when I looked immensely bored, but rather came over as he fished in his pocket for Werther's candy to give to me. What he needed my help with was folding the chairs and tables, putting them away and re-setting the small sanctuary for Sunday service. It came to be our tradition and it signaled to me that the prison break was on and Care and Share was over.

What was better though, were the talks we had. I don't know if it was his accent or the quiet, kind way he talked or the fact that he seemed to understand me . . . maybe all of them . . . but I could listen to Ron for hours. He talked to me about the time of World War II, how he had fought in it and what life was like then. He remembered such vivid details and could weave them together in an engaging tale. He told me about life as a boy in England, coming to America and meeting his one true love, Audrey. I will never forget those times or Ron.

One of the last times I saw him was early in my missionary calling when I was back home for a Sunday service. They told me that Ron had cancer and the doctors had not given him much time to live. Then they asked me to pray for him along with the elders and leaders of the church. It was one of the first times I had ever been asked to pray for physical healing in front of people and honestly, through my grief at the bad news, I was not all that "faith filled." I did pray, however, and anoint him with oil. God must have taken some of the love that Ron and I had shared in our hours together when I was a boy and poured it back down on him from heaven because two weeks later my mother called me and gave me the update: Ron was cancer-free! No one deserved it more than he did.

In the beginning of this book, I said I wanted to focus on three main characters: Samuel, Saul and David. I mentioned how Saul was old enough to be David's father and maybe even a very young grandfather at forty years older than he. Samuel was quite a

35

bit older than David, sixty-two years older, in fact. David was only fifteen years old when Samuel anointed him as king over Israel at the house of his father Jesse. David had encounters with both these men in his life, but they had profoundly different effects on him. One was the age of a grandfather and a leader in Israel, the other, a king and a literal father-in-law. Samuel saw the potential in a teenage shepherd and poured the transformative oil over him, releasing a mantle to rule. Yet Saul competed with David over and again, and in fits of rage even tried to kill him on several occasions.

The actions of Samuel and Saul represent starkly different options for the leaders of the older generation. You can be a Samuel to the Davids coming along behind and pour the anointing oil, or you can be a Saul and compete with them, seeking to pin them to the wall with your spear.

Just as Samuel poured precious oil onto David for his generation, I think Ron was certainly a Samuel in my life. I often wonder what Samuel's eyes must have looked like as he beheld David for the first time. Imagine being a seventy-seven-year-old prophet who had led a nation and who was coming off what must have felt like great failure both with his own sons and with Saul. In the midst of that, he is instructed to anoint a new king. He sees the logical choice before him in Eliab as mentioned in 1 Samuel 16:6, but the Lord says, "no." He goes through all the sons of Jesse and one after another the Lord says no to all of them. Then this man first laid his eyes upon a fifteen-year-old boy, fresh from the fields. No wonder God had to tell Samuel not to look as man does, but rather with eyes of faith.

When I think of that first interaction, I can't help but remember my first interaction with Ron. He could have judged me and written me off as some hyperactive, annoying kid that he wanted nothing to do with. He could have pinned me to a wall like a Saul with strict discipline and a harsh regimen, telling me that was what I needed. Or he could have ignored me altogether and pretended I didn't exist. This would have been the Saul way. But instead, he loved me and poured the precious oil of his time and love onto me.

He had an impact on my life that goes beyond what he may ever be aware of.

When I consider the Samuels of our generation I have great respect for them. I don't know where we would be in the earth or in the Body of Christ without them. But for all those that I am aware of, I am also aware that there are countless others that no one knows about, just like Ron. They are the hidden, unsung heroes on their knees in bedrooms, prayer closets and living rooms all over the world, praying us through. They are the grandmothers and grandfathers who have shed their tears in bitter watches of the night and paid the price in intercession that we might know and begin to walk in our calling.

But just as a young heart full of zeal and fervor does not necessarily a David make, neither do years or life experience necessarily a Samuel make. Life experience and true wisdom and authority from the Lord are not the same thing. It is true that the generations need to come together, but it has to be rightly aligned. Davids need to know a true Samuel from a Saul just like the Samuels need to know a true David from zealous rebellion. If not, there will be a lot more dysfunction and disappointment.

As a David writing this, I am blessed to have a very real and present Samuel in my life in Apostle Barbara Yoder. But, I am aware that many young Davids reading this do not necessarily have someone to look to. What does it look like to be a Samuel or a Saul? What qualifies you as a Samuel? What are some characteristics that should mark the life of someone who has precious oil that this coming David generation needs? Before we get to the assignment of Samuel and the process for pouring the oil, let's look at some character traits of a true Samuel and juxtapose them next to the traits of a Saul in the next chapter.

Samuels Are Brought Forth in Glory

The first character trait that I believe must mark the life of a true Samuel is being greatly impacted and touched by the Glory of God. The Bible speaks of Samuel encountering the Lord in a time when the heavens were tightly shut up (in 1 Samuel 3). God called him and transformed him in a moment of glory from a sweet child who served in the Tabernacle to the prophet of God known throughout the whole land. The encounter that Samuel had with the Lord was the thing that birthed him into his God-given destiny. It placed upon him the mantle under which he operated his whole life.

If you are to bring something to birth, you have to first be pregnant. One encounter from God can so impregnate you that you birth and bring forth an anointing that can last a lifetime. The mark of any true Samuel is this genuine encounter with God. Out of that encounter comes transformation and the impartation of the precious oil.

You must encounter God *for yourself* in order to get such results. Samuel's mother Hannah had prayed and cried out in the place of desperation, been heard by God and had consecrated Samuel to the Lord, but that wasn't enough. Samuel had to encounter God for himself. It had to go beyond the prayers, desperation and obedience of his mother.

Words of life experience and wisdom are good, but words that drip with the sweet fragrance from heaven are much better! The words brought forth from the storehouses of Glory are worth more than a hundred years of street smarts and worldly knowledge.

Let me pause here to say something to the Davids: I do believe that although not all who are grey-haired and full of years and life experience are Samuels to whom we need to be listening and from whom we need to be receiving in a spiritual sense, we still need to honor every one of our elders. We have somehow lost this in society as a whole. I don't want what I am saying to be misconstrued. We need to recreate in our generation and the generations to come a culture of honor. In fact, the whole of this book is meant to help create a culture of honor that unites us all. I will say it again: Not all elders have equal function to impart spiritually, but all deserve honor. We should not cast honor off even in the midst of "chewing the meat and spitting out the bones," so to speak.

Samuels Have a Track Record of Results

The Bible says: *"So Samuel grew, and the LORD was with him and let none of his words fall to the ground"* (1 Samuel 3:19, NKJV).

For the Davids looking for a Samuel, you cannot go to just anyone. As I said, all elders deserve respect, but not all can or should impart to you spiritually. Some people can be just as wounded and "messed up" at eighty-five as they were at fifteen. You want to be receiving from someone who has a track record of obedience and the fruit of results directly correlated to that obedience.

Now, the track record I am speaking of does not have to be fifty years long. It doesn't even have to be fifteen years. Try not to put such things in a box or use a legalistic measuring rod. What I am saying is to carefully evaluate things before you open yourself up to receive from someone. There is power in the laying on of hands (see Hebrews 6)—for better or for worse. You don't want an impartation from the wrong Samuel. After all, impartation tends to stick.

It is important to know that you are connecting with someone who is a greater authority and measure of faith than your own. You need to be stretched and grow in order to fulfill what God has called you to. Does the potential Samuel have a track record of obedience in his or her life, a life lived in surrender to righteousness and holiness? Has the person been obedient to the covenant of marriage or to a single lifestyle lived in holiness? Has he or she been committed to a local church and served there with consistency? Don't just look at spiritual things, look at the practical too.

Ask yourself the question, "Do I want my life to look like that?" Then after you have evaluated the foundations of the person's life, look at the results. Has the person led a successful business? (This is especially important if that is the area of endeavor you feel called to.) Has the person's ministry increased in anointing? What was the fruit or outcome of strategic assignments given by God?

I am not saying you will necessarily find all of these factors in perfect order. People are people and no one is perfect. But this is a starting grid to begin to evaluate if you have found a Samuel.

Samuels Will Pour Everything They Have Out to You

We read in Scripture that,

Samuel took the horn of oil and anointed him in the midst of his brothers; and the Spirit of the LORD came upon David from that day forward. So Samuel arose and went to Ramah. (1 Samuel 16:13, NKJV)

Scholars say that a horn of oil contained from four to seven liters of oil. That is from one to almost two gallons of oil! The person pouring the oil would not just pour a little bit; he would pour the entire contents on the one being anointed. That oil would flow from the head all the way down to the rest of the body of whomever was being anointed. When Samuel anointed David, he poured out all that he had in his horn.

A true Samuel doesn't hold anything back. All the life experience, all the love and kindness, all the wisdom and more is poured forth freely onto the Davids of the present and coming generation. God is not stingy! Neither should the Samuels be.

I just saw again a movie which was was based on a book I had read as a child, *The Count of Monte Cristo*, by Alexandre Dumas. This writer was a genius who wrote other great works such as *The Three Musketeers*, *The Man in the Iron Mask* series and more. Some of you may know the story. There are two friends, one of whom betrays the other. The one who is betrayed is thrown into a horrible pit-like prison on a remote island in the sea. In the midst of his imprisonment he despairs of everything including life itself. He comes so low in his anguish and bitterness of heart that he decides one day to take his very life. It doesn't work and he is left even lower in pain and agony. In the midst of all of this, one day, out of the blue, another prisoner pops up literally out of the ground of his prison cell! It is Abbé Faria who has been imprisoned in the same jail for many years. He was tunneling underneath the surface in hopes of escaping to his freedom. Instead he ended up in the cell of Edmond Dantes the young man who has lost all hope.

What ensues next is one of the most powerful depictions of the heart of a true Samuel I have seen captured yet. Abbé Faria pulls Edmond not only out of despair, but out of his cell! He leads him back through the tunnels he has dug over many years of hardship and pain and brings him to his cell, which to Edmond feels like another country altogether. The fellowship and comradery that takes place is amazing to behold, but more powerful yet is the impartation that Abbé Faria gives to Edmond.

At the time that they meet, Edmond does not read or know anything of literature, the arts or warfare at all. As the two continue every day to tunnel, Abbé Faria teaches Edmond everything he knows. He holds nothing back. He teaches Edmond economics, poetry, literature, other languages and also warfare tactics and swordsmanship. I was very moved by this portrayal, which to me perfectly encapsulates much of what I am trying to communicate here. And the most powerful portrayal of all was in the end, when Abbé Faria gave his very life for Edmond's freedom. Edmond was able to escape from the prison and he went on to become one of the wealthiest people in all the world.

This story provides such a powerful depiction of the heart of a Samuel, who will give all he or she has to others, empowering them to prosper. This is God's heart and also the heart of a true Samuel.

Now let's look at some of the characteristics of a Saul, so that we can be aware and wise as we move forward.

Chapter 4

UNDERSTANDING THE SAUL STRUCTURE

Unmasking this Ungodly Spirit

Ah, King Saul. His stories and antics are enough to fill up any daytime soap opera or talk show and then some. You can almost just hear Dr. Phil talking to him, "Saul, what's all this repressed aggression? Why throw the spear Saul? Why?" Was it insane jealousy about David killing more enemies than he had? Or was he slinging his spear in order to create a new wall decoration—out of David? At any rate, Saul was quite the colorful character.

What happened to Saul and the nation was a result of sin, poor choices and the rejection of God's leadership over the nation. Samuel warned them over and again about it and grieved bitterly. Samuel knew what the people were asking for. He knew they were exchanging being led by the very glory of God for a system of men. When he inquired of the Lord about it, God made things very clear. He spoke to Samuel:

> *And the LORD said to Samuel, "Heed the voice of the people in all that they say to you; for they have not rejected you, but they have rejected Me, that I should not reign over them. According to all the works which they have done since the day that I brought them up out of Egypt, even to this day— with which they have forsaken Me and served other gods—so they are doing to you also. Now therefore, heed their voice.*

However, you shall solemnly forewarn them, and show them the behavior of the king who will reign over them."
(1 Samuel 8:7–9, NKJV)

What Saul represents more than anything is a structure. Samuel did as the Lord told him and began the process of setting this new structure in place; a structure from its inception that displeased the Lord. They were taking the honor they would normally give to the Lord and putting it onto a man. Samuel describes to them what will happen:

And he said, "This will be the behavior of the king who will reign over you: He will take your sons and appoint them for his own chariots and to be his horsemen, and some will run before his chariots. He will appoint captains over his thousands and captains over his fifties, will set some to plow his ground and reap his harvest, and some to make his weapons of war and equipment for his chariots. He will take your daughters to be perfumers, cooks, and bakers. And he will take the best of your fields, your vineyards, and your olive groves, and give them to his servants. He will take a tenth of your grain and your vintage, and give it to his officers and servants. And he will take your male servants, your female servants, your finest young men, and your donkeys, and put them to his work. He will take a tenth of your sheep. And you will be his servants. And you will cry out in that day because of your king whom you have chosen for yourselves, and the LORD will not hear you in that day."
(1 Samuel 8:11–18, NKJV)

The things that would normally be dedicated to God as holy would now belong to the king, Samuel warned them. Their sons and daughters, their fields, their servants, their tithes! But Scripture says they refused to listen.

As I read the entire story it's hard not to feel a little sorry for Saul. He seems to be a genuine person, especially in the beginning, and he is one whom the Lord uses. There are several instances of the Spirit of the Lord coming on Saul powerfully. He leads the army in victory, he prophesies, he listens to Samuel. But if something is wrong at the beginning, chances are it is not going to get better as it progresses. Three times Samuel warns Israel of their folly, even on the occasion of the inauguration of the new king. You can read these accounts in 1 Samuel 8:11–18; 10:19 and 12:16–17.

In the Lord's benevolence, however he still loves his people. He still cares for them and sees their pain. He has Samuel anoint Saul, because he has a destiny and purpose for him:

> *Tomorrow about this time I will send you a man from the land of Benjamin, and you shall anoint him commander over My people Israel, that he may save My people from the hand of the Philistines; for I have looked upon My people, because their cry has come to Me.* (1 Samuel 9:16, NKJV)

But Saul misses his destiny when he disobeys the Lord, which makes the Lord actually regret having made him king (see 1 Samuel 15:11). For me, this is one of the most interesting verses of all. The Lord regrets something? How can that be possible? The New King James version of the text renders it as, "I greatly regret...." You know the story; the anointing departs from Saul and an evil spirit comes in place of it.

To once have had an anointing and then to lose it makes you a very dangerous person. You resemble a wily fox lying in wait. I think of what Jesus said:

> *If therefore the light that is in you is darkness, how great is that darkness!* (Matthew 6:23, NKJV)

This is what happened to Saul. The glory that had once been upon him in the form of an anointing to lead had now been exchanged for another power. As I read the Scripture I can see that it's almost as if he became equally as enraged and delusional as he was once zealous for God.

The results of this unholy exchange are the signposts we will look at as we evaluate the Saul structure. This is the structure that

God has been pulling down in the Church over the past several decades. We have come to a crucial point in this process, and now the generations need to work together to accomplish the full removal of it. Samuel and David both had parts to play in removing Saul and fulfilling the word of the Lord.

What must be removed? Let's look at some of the characteristics of a Saul structure. This is not a comprehensive rendering, just some points I feel are necessary to highlight.

Saul's Armor

We all know the account of when David was about to fight Goliath. He goes in to Saul for some kingly advice and Saul dresses him in a suit of armor that does not fit. Notice that this parallel runs throughout the Saul structure; he tried to robe David in the arm of the flesh. It didn't fit. God wanted to work the miracle. This pattern can be seen at the very inception of Saul's reign because of the sin of the people in even asking for a king. It's not that this was Saul's fault, but what I am saying is that it shows the establishment of a structure—the structure of the arm of the flesh. This pattern never stopped. Ultimately it caused the beginning of Saul's unraveling as a leader.

This reliance on the flesh is how the Saul structure works to get us away from the Glory. It may seem innocent and even reasonable at first, but in the end the results are death. We need to realize that even what seem to be reasonable good intentions, apart from the Glory, are deceptive. We will discuss this further; one of the main aspects of the Saul structure is a deceptive spirit.

Here is an example of what I mean when I say that Saul moved in the arm of the flesh and made that his place of strength:

> *Then he waited seven days, according to the time set by Samuel. But Samuel did not come to Gilgal; and the people were scattered from him. So Saul said, "Bring a burnt offering and peace offerings here to me." And he offered the burnt offering. Now it happened, as soon as he had finished*

45

presenting the burnt offering, that Samuel came; and Saul
went out to meet him, that he might greet him.
  And Samuel said, "What have you done?"
  Saul said, "When I saw that the people were scattered
from me, and that you did not come within the days
appointed, and that the Philistines gathered together at
Michmash, then I said, 'The Philistines will now come down
on me at Gilgal, and I have not made supplication to the
LORD.' Therefore, I felt compelled, and offered a burnt
offering." (1 Samuel 13:8–12, NKJV)

The account in Scripture goes on to tell how Samuel declares to Saul that he has made a fatal mistake and that the kingdom will be taken away from him and given to another. Samuel says this act of the flesh and disobedience does not reflect God's heart. Moving in his own strength instead of God's strength—it will end up costing Saul everything.

In looking at the scriptural account, it's easy to see how Saul panicked and did what he felt to be reasonable and logical. "Reasonable," "logical," "makes sense"—these can often result in death sentences for someone! Everything we do must be birthed from the Glory. Jesus said in John 3:6 that "The flesh gives birth to flesh." Regardless of what place in society you find yourself in as you read this, this truth applies. Whether you feel called as a David or Samuel to business, media, education, religion or another place in society, what you do must be born of the Spirit of God. Otherwise, you will ultimately fail. The arm of flesh will fail you every time.

Saul's act here was not born of the Glory. His actions were born of fear, rebellion and arrogance: fear of the people, who were beginning to scatter; rebellion against the Lord's right order of things, because this action belonged to Samuel and not to him; and arrogance, because he stepped into a role and mantle that he was not ordained or ready for.

This is how Saul's armor, his suit of strength operates. It is not a person, it is a structure born of the flesh that costs the very glory of God.

Saul Pleases People and Calls it Sacrifice

Fear pervades this Saul structure. Fear is insidious. It produces all kinds of bad fruit and makes you a slave (see, for example, Galatians 4:7). Saul was becoming more and more bound to his fear of the people.

This act of disobedience marks the time when God's final judgment was released through Samuel against Saul's kingdom and rule. This fear-born disobedience led to deception. The prophet Samuel had told Saul that God remembered the suffering of his people and his hand is against the Amalekites. Through Samuel, the Glory commanded Saul to wipe everything out and remove it from the land:

> *This is what the Lord Almighty says. "I will punish the Amalekites for what they did to Israel when they waylaid them as they came up from Egypt. Now go, attack the Amalekites and totally destroy all that belongs to them. Do not spare them; put to death men and women, children and infants, cattle and sheep, camels and donkeys."* (1 Samuel 15:2–3, NIV)

Saul went to battle and he was victorious . . . but not in the eyes of the Lord. He had disobeyed the clear command of the Lord. This was his fatal mistake:

> *So when Samuel rose early in the morning to meet Saul, it was told Samuel, saying, "Saul went to Carmel, and indeed, he set up a monument for himself; and he has gone on around, passed by, and gone down to Gilgal." Then Samuel went to Saul, and Saul said to him, "Blessed are you of the LORD! I have performed the commandment of the LORD."*
> *But Samuel said, "What then is this bleating of the sheep in my ears, and the lowing of the oxen which I hear?"*
> *And Saul said, "They have brought them from the Amalekites; for the people spared the best of the sheep and*

the oxen, to sacrifice to the LORD *your God; and the rest we have utterly destroyed."* (1 Samuel 15:12–15, NJKV)

"The people" spared the best, Saul said. When you confront a Saul structure, be ready for blame reassignment. It was Saul's responsibility to lead the people and fulfill the assignment from the Lord. Instead he feared the people rather than God and tried to cover his rebellion by sweeping it under the rug of "holy sacrifice." Again, deception is hard at work here. Saul reassigns, redirects and covers over his sin. The prophet didn't buy it. As the story goes on, we see that the kingdom and the Glory are ripped from Saul, all because Saul tried to please the people more than he tried to please God.

A Saul structure will always seek to please people before fulfilling an assignment of the Lord. A Saul structure will fear losing, offending or displeasing people. The priorities are always out of alignment and the Glory is the last thing to be revered. It all gets placed under the banner of "sacrifice" when that is not what the Lord was asking for; he was asking for obedience.

As people and followers of the Lord Jesus, we have to have our priorities straight. This man-pleasing pattern can cost us everything! If you are in business, do you do the unethical thing just because someone else is, or because you can make more money? In church, do you water down the message because you may lose people and their weekly tithes? In media, do you compromise and film and release things that you know are not right because it is what the current trends require? We cannot give in to this structure; it will rob us of the Glory and ultimately, of our God-given inheritance.

Saul Holds onto Position Long after the Anointing Has Gone

Not long after this incident, God told Samuel to rise up and anoint a new breed, someone who would be after his own heart. From the moment that Samuel released the prophecy when the corner of his robe tore (see 1 Sam. 15:27–28), God was setting up a new administration. Samuel arose and went to anoint David and the new administration began. From that point on, though no one knew him yet, David began to increase and Saul to decrease. The anointing

48

of David occurred among his brothers; it was not a public anointing. But even though it was just done in a private setting among a few, the power of it began to work immediately.

And so we come to a unique point in Saul, David and Samuel's lives. God had torn the kingdom from Saul and given it to David, but Saul was still king. David had the anointing, but Saul had the position. David had fresh oil, but Saul had all the resources and power.

I can't help but feel that this is where we are in many respects in the Body of Christ in the present day. A new move is rising up and gaining momentum, but it is still so small. There are countless nameless and faceless prophets and apostles that no one knows about, whom the Lord has anointed. They are in Africa and Asia and South America and the United States and everywhere. They are in the caves of obscurity just as David was in 1 Samuel 22– –running from a structure that seems to want to kill them!

I have great respect for churches all over the world. I believe in the power of the Church both in a regional and a local sense. But, even though I love the Church, much of what I observe, especially in North America, appears to be a Saul structure. I am not saying this from a mean spirit, nor am I seeking to stir up negativity as I write this. But at some point we have to admit that the anointing has left the building just like Elvis! What I mean is that the anointing and power of the Acts 2 church does not seem to be present anymore. No one is getting saved, healed or delivered, and our society by and large is not being impacted by the power of God through the Church. Yet we keep the machine going. We keep the ninety-minute, entertaining "wheel of moolah" spinning. We sing to the tune of fellowship and trendy coffee shops. We have our black-light, multimedia worship services where people sit and talk and maybe listen with lattes in their hands. We have huge 5,000- and 10,000-member churches, but we see little to no change happening in the world. Position, but no power. Name, but no anointing. Organization, but nothing organic or growing.

Even though it would seem that Saul should feel secure and not worried at all, a growing movement was happening underneath his very feet. Shockwaves of a new administration began to threaten him and his kingdom began to crumble. This drove him to a certain level of insanity which was fueled by fear, paranoia and jealousy.

If you want to be on the cutting edge of what God is doing, you need to be aware that the religious and political structure will oppose you. This is the Saul structure that warred against the house of David for many years and sought to wipe it out. You will most definitely be dodging javelins as they are thrown at you!

In most cases, the assaults won't be overt or obvious. They will come covertly, from underneath the surface, dripping with deception. In Saul's story, we see that not only had the Glory departed from Saul, but in place, a distressing spirit came (see 1 Samuel 16:14–23). Saul called for a minstrel and this is how David first came to him. In fact, the Scripture says that Saul loved David greatly and David became his armor bearer. And when David would play his music, the evil spirit would leave Saul. You see, Saul didn't start out by throwing javelins at David.

Many times when I read the Scripture, I think of the evil spirit that was upon Saul as the impetus for him to want to kill David. Even though that was surely a part of it, I want to suggest something else. Could it have been the jealousy that drove Saul mad? Could it have been when he felt his position threatened that he crossed the line into a murderous spirit?

Look at the progression in Scripture. Saul and David connected and formed a relationship. David came back and forth to the king to play for him. Somewhere along the line, Israel was attacked by the Philistines and David killed their champion. This caused Saul to give David his daughter and also place him in higher and higher levels in his military forces. David's fame began to spread and *the people* that Saul had so been controlled by start to shift their favor. This jealously grew into insanity and eventually murder in Saul's heart, because David threatened his position.

The Saul structure does not want to give up control of its position. When it feels threatened, you can know that the javelins are in the air. The good news is that ultimately David does not have to deal with Saul; he only has to remain faithful and *endure the process.*

Allow God to Deal with Saul

This is the last point I will make in this chapter, but I believe that it is a vital one. As I said earlier, both Samuel and David have a part to play in bringing down this Saul structure. Ultimately however, it is not the strength of man or will of man which accomplishes that. If it was, that would be *replacing Saul with Saul.*

Jesus said that Satan could not cast out Satan (see Matthew 12:26). So it is with this structure. You cannot bring it down in the same spirit that it operates in. You cannot get a chip on your shoulder and think that you now get to become the judge. I have seen this way too many times, and it is completely ineffective.

Imagine a host of Davids and Samuels with chips on their shoulders and anger in their hearts taking this on. Imagine them barging into churches and businesses and yelling at the top of their lungs about the changes that are needed. Imagine them talking and gossiping about churches and leaders and people as self-appointed judges, full of gusto and zeal in their "holy quest" to "pull down Saul's structure." Unfortunately, this is actually not that hard to imagine. A lot that is done in the name of "prophetic ministry" is nothing more than the flesh at work—and it stinks.

If you want to take new territory, you have to have eyes and hearts that are of an excellent spirit, a spirit like Joshua and Caleb had. You know the story so well. Of all the spies that went into the land, they were the only ones who returned with a good report. That passage of Scripture reads:

> *But My servant Caleb, because he has a different spirit in him and has followed Me fully, I will bring into the land*

where he went, and his descendants shall inherit it.
(Numbers 14:24, NKJV)

If we want to bring about a true change we have to have a different spirit, a heart and an attitude that is like Joshua and Caleb's. You cannot bring change by the means of anger, annoyance and rebellion.

David had to learn this lesson. When he was still hiding from Saul who was yet again trying to kill him, Saul's search for David brought him into a cave in which David was hiding. While Saul was, shall we say, "indisposed," David cut the corner off his robe:

> *Then the men of David said to him, "This is the day of which the LORD said to you, 'Behold, I will deliver your enemy into your hand, that you may do to him as it seems good to you.'" And David arose and secretly cut off a corner of Saul's robe. Now it happened afterward that David's heart troubled him because he had cut Saul's robe. And he said to his men, "The LORD forbid that I should do this thing to my master, the LORD's anointed, to stretch out my hand against him, seeing he is the anointed of the LORD."* (1 Samuel 24:4, NKJV)

David was right to repent of his actions. Had he killed Saul, Jerusalem would most likely not be called, "The city of David" today! David's heart was tested and even though he didn't perfectly pass, he made it through the test. It may have looked like a small thing, but in cutting off the corner of Saul's kingly robe, David was symbolically cutting off his authority. It was not David's place to do that; it was God's. God is the one who sets up and puts down.

Likewise, in this process we are in, our hearts will be tested. I want to encourage you; if you see a Saul structure around you, do not deal with it in the flesh. Pray, fast, humble yourself. Allow God to put things in order. You worry about your character, and God will take care of the rest.

Now that we have defined Samuels and Sauls, let's look at the process for activating Samuel to anoint David. Arise Samuels! Now is your time. You are vitally important!

Chapter 5

SAMUELS, ARISE!

Time for the Older Generation to Pour the Oil

Henry Ford said, "If I had asked people what they wanted, they would have said, 'Faster horses.'" Life is like that isn't it? We constantly have to come to grips with different ways in which the comfortable "status quo" is the enemy of the uncomfortable "could be." We rarely ever change things unless something forces us to do so. There is something about our nature that accepts things; even if they are bad or mediocre. We rationalize and become comforted by the knowledge that we are aware of what *is.* What *could be* is the part that often scares us—although it also excites us. The potential for the future lies in the "could be."

I believe that Samuel found himself in such a place after his last encounter with Saul (1 Samuel 15). He had known what could happen if the Israelites' demand for a king was realized, and his worst fears had come true. He was in his home in Ramah mourning for Saul, stuck in the status quo. Saul had failed and I would imagine that in some way perhaps Samuel felt that he had failed too. His sons had not walked in his ways, the king he had appointed had rebelled and he was getting very old. He must have been in that place of mourning for at least a little while, given the way God spoke to him:

> *Now the LORD said to Samuel, "How long will you mourn for Saul, seeing I have rejected him from reigning over Israel? Fill your horn with oil, and go; I am sending you to Jesse the Bethlehemite. For I have provided Myself a king among his sons." (1 Samuel 16:1, NKJV)*

Samuel might have felt like his mourning was not all that long, but apparently God disagreed. He told him to get up and get out of the place of mourning and despair. It was as if he was saying, "Seek out a brave new future together with me! There is something new I want to do that is far beyond what you have known." God was trying to expand Samuel's horizons to see that there was something more than just faster horses. It is interesting to think back to the very beginning for Samuel. When the Lord called him, the word of the Lord was that God would do something new which would "make people's ears tingle" (see 1 Samuel 3:11). Samuel had seen a part of that already come to pass through his own ministry. But, God was getting ready to birth something again.

Normally that birthing happens out of the context of great darkness and failure. This past season in the earth has been pretty brutal. I know of many people who feel that they have been beaten down by the past season. It's not only the older generation who feel this way although, as you can imagine, it has hit them very hard. Even though many younger people have been struggling as well, it is fair to say it's not the same for a David as for a Samuel. As a young person myself, I know that whatever I have gone through, as hard as it may have been, I have a lot of my life still ahead of me. My greatest accomplishments are not in my past but in my future.

On the other hand, many leaders in the older generation, leaders of churches, businesses and more, feel that they have diminished and lost much in the past decade. They feel as though the past season is sitting on them like a heavy burden. They may be asking themselves the question, "how will I have the strength to build again?" It might feel easier to stay and remain in mourning than to arise and build again—this time also not to build alone, but along with the younger generation, which poses its own challenges.

I want to be careful to pause here to make sure that I don't exclude people who are reading this who are not leaders of churches, businesses and the like. There may be some reading this who do not feel a sense of spiritual or financial stress or burden, although they may feel it in a physical sense, in their bodies. They may feel they

55

are not in any kind of mourning, but rather are limited by what is going on in their health. I want to say to you that I believe that a fresh wind of strength is coming to you, as well. You are going to begin to feel the power of the Lord in your body. You will rise up again. Your energy is going to return, your strength is going to return and you will step into your purpose for this very moment!

Whether you fall into one of the categories I have described or something totally different, this is such an important time. In the midst of your feelings and what you may be going through, God is again doing a new thing! He is breaking through into new territory just as Henry Ford did. Horses were great for their time, but cars have taken us a quantum leap into the future. We are about to take a quantum leap into a new paradigm—the generations working together. I believe that the Samuels of our time have a huge and vital part to play in this. They are the ones who will pour the oil onto the coming generations and see the greatest move of God in history come forth.

What does that look like? What are the steps in this process? How do the Samuels arise out of a very hard season even as the ancient Samuel did?

Arise Out of the Old Season

I heard someone ask once, "Why are people always prophesying 'a new season' every ten seconds?" I honestly couldn't help myself when they asked me that, and I laughed out loud! I quickly tried to compose myself and answer the question that he was very serious about. I told him I understood his question and that I feel that certainly some prophetic words could come up a level. But, I also told him that I believe that the very nature of the prophetic is to declare new things all the time. The Bible says that the spirit of prophecy is the testimony of Jesus.

Jesus is the author of creativity, and he is therefore always doing something new. It is our job to take notice and then participate. In order to participate in something new you always have to leave behind something old. It is a dichotomy of sorts and can be difficult at times because most of the time, *we love what we have*. We are connected to it because we participated in creating and maintaining it. We were emotionally and financially invested in it; we put our time and effort into it.

That is why Samuel was mourning for Saul. He was invested in Saul! He wanted Saul to be a success and for the full purpose of God's heart and plan for Saul to come forth. He wasn't waiting in the wings for Saul to fail.

So many in the older generation have been a part of what God did in the past. They were connected, invested and fully committed to it. They demonstrated faithfulness to the move of God in a way that the younger generation must learn from. That is admirable and I honor that. But, when God begins to do something new, or when the anointing leaves, you have to be willing to move with God. If you are in a Saul structure and do not arise out of it when God tells you to, you will get stuck. Not only will you get stuck in an old structure, you will die in an old structure. I am not speaking of physical death, but rather of spiritual and emotional death.

From the moment Saul was rejected as king over Israel, his rule and reign became a structure of death. It was never going to get any better. Some of us hang on to what we have, thinking that somehow things are going to get better. While that may be true in some cases, in the vast majority it is not. When God says, "Go!" we must obey.

Sometimes the thing that stops us from following the call to "arise and go" is fear. Fear can be crippling at times and can make us feel as if something has us by the throat. You feel that if you even make a move, you are going to get jumped on and injured in some way. The Saul structure operates in fear, control and deceit. Samuel himself encountered this and it was his first response to the Lord when God spoke:

> *And Samuel said, "How can I go? If Saul hears it, he will kill me."* (1 Samuel 16:2, NKJV)

I love God's response to Samuel. He doesn't dismiss Samuel's concern; he actually works with him in the midst of it. Samuel had a very legitimate concern! Basically, he was committing treason. He was conducting a coup d'état against the reign of Saul. If Saul had heard about it and had known what Samuel was doing, he, David and David's whole house would have been killed. So God responded with a plan:

> But the LORD said, "Take a heifer with you, and say, 'I have come to sacrifice to the LORD.' Then invite Jesse to the sacrifice, and I will show you what you shall do; you shall anoint for Me the one I name to you." (1 Samuel 16:2–3, NKJV)

If you find yourself in a Saul structure and feel afraid to move, know that God has a plan for you. It will be different for everyone, but there is a path out of that place of paralyzing fear, forward into victory and fresh assignment. Fear is incompatible with obedience. We have to rise above fear and move with bold confidence. I love this quote by Nelson Mandela:

> I learned that courage was not the absence of fear, but the triumph over it. The brave man is not he who does not feel afraid, but he who conquers that fear.

Your David is waiting for you on the other side of bold and courageous action.

Look with New Eyes

Once we arise out of grief and fear, we then need to look with new eyes. Where connecting the generations is concerned, we need to enter into a new paradigm altogether, or we will more than likely have the same results. A supernatural transaction needs to happen, bringing with it new eyes that see and a heart that feels alive.

Samuels are going to have to see and look past a lot of things in working with Davids. Looking with the natural eyes may leave you uninterested, frustrated, fearful or more. If you look with the eyes of the spirit, you will begin to see something altogether "other." This "other" is the often-undefined, raw material of a life that possesses untapped potential. That is what Samuels are meant to see and call forth.

When Samuel arrived at the home of Jesse and the sons started appearing before him, he was still thinking of faster horses. His concept needed to shift.

> *"Sanctify yourselves, and come with me to the sacrifice."*
> *Then he consecrated Jesse and his sons, and invited them to*
> *the sacrifice.*
> *So it was, when they came, that he looked at Eliab*
> *and said, "Surely the LORD's anointed is before Him!" But*
> *the LORD said to Samuel, "Do not look at his appearance or*
> *at his physical stature, because I have refused him. For the*
> *LORD does not see as man sees; for man looks at the outward*
> *appearance, but the LORD looks at the heart."* (1 Samuel
> 16:5–6, NKJV)

When Samuel beheld Eliab, he was still in the mindset of looking for another Saul. He thought, *here is a horse that can run fast! Perhaps even faster than the previous model!* God then transported Samuel into a new paradigm at the speed of light and the word of the Lord broke through. It was as if God was saying, *Ever heard of a "car," Samuel? Let me show you one...*

In a sense, what I am saying is that you have got to start looking with the eyes of a futurist. Here is the definition of a futurist:

FUTURIST:
(1) An adherent of futurism. (2) A person who studies the future and makes predictions about it based on current trends.

Now, apply that definition to people's lives, to moves of the Holy Spirit, to burgeoning ministries and endeavors and the like.

When you observe these, you observe them from a perspective not of the "now," but rather of their future potential.

Let me add also the ingredient of *redemption*. From a purely definitive perspective, to be a futurist means to look at trends as they are. Sometimes that is very good, but sometimes it is not. There are good trends and not-so-good trends. To be futurists as God would have us be, we need to look at positive trends and nurture them. Conversely, we need to look at negative trends and call those things that are *not now* as though they *are*.

A futurist doesn't see the "now" or even think in the parameters of "now." They look and think far beyond "what is," the comfort and familiarity of the present, and gaze into the realm of "magnificent possibility." Some of the Davids that God will bring before you will not look like a horse . . . or a car . . . or anything you have ever seen before! But within the broken vessel lies a vast treasure for those who have eyes to *value it*.

Dr. Mahesh Chavda once gave me a very good example of this. I was asking him how he thinks about healing and faith. He told me that when he approaches people, he doesn't look at them as they are now—in a wheelchair, deaf, blind, etc. He said that when he looks at them, he looks at them through the lens of Glory. In the Glory, there is no need, lack, disease, or anything of the sort. He said, "I look into their future and agree now with the healing they have already received through Christ." What a powerful example! Samuels, as you behold your Davids, look through the lens of Glory at their destiny and agree in the here and now with it!

Look with new eyes and pour the oil.

The "No Competition" Zone

The final point I will share in this chapter for Samuels is about living in what I call the "no competition zone."

This past summer, we had a prophetic conference and one of the speakers we invited was James Goll. I have great respect for

James Goll. I think only time will tell of the true impact that he has had on the world and especially the charismatic movement of the church. His books, teachings and more have set so many foundation stones in place and brought definition to much that was only theory and concept.

James spoke at the conference and stayed over to preach on Sunday morning. As he began, he stated that he'd had a dream the night before and he wanted to demonstrate what he saw. He proceeded to call me, Apostle Barbara Yoder and two other people who work with us up to the front. He had Apostle Barbara and myself stand next to each other on one side and the two other people stand across from us. He then began to sing a song about us all working together: a lead pastor (me), an apostle (Apostle Barbara Yoder), a prophet, and a prophetic intercessor. He then sang and prophesied: "I have never seen it like this before! Unity, in a "no competition zone."

That has really stayed with me and I have been chewing on it for some time. What does that mean for us as a new breed in a new movement?

Unfortunately, as you look over past moves of God, sometimes the past move of God criticizes and persecutes the current move of God. I think some of that is due to misunderstanding and a lack of communication over some of the new things that are being poured out. But even though that may be true and it does come into play, I think more times than not, the criticism comes from competition.

Looking back for a moment at the Saul structure, there was certainly competition there. When David began to gain fame and notoriety, they began to sing songs about him as was common in that time:

> *Now it had happened as they were coming home, when David was returning from the slaughter of the Philistine, that the women had come out of all the cities of Israel, singing and dancing, to meet King Saul, with tambourines, with joy, and*

with musical instruments. So the women sang as they danced, and said:

> *"Saul has slain his thousands,*
> *And David his ten thousands."*

Then Saul was very angry, and the saying displeased him; and he said, "They have ascribed to David ten thousands, and to me they have ascribed only thousands. Now what more can he have but the kingdom?" So Saul eyed David from that day forward. (1 Samuel 18:6–9, NKJV)

David's success brought about such jealousy and anger in Saul. The heart of a true Samuel does not respond this way.

Apostle Barbara Yoder said something to me recently that was extremely profound. She said, "I feel that at this point in my journey, my main assignment is to give everything away to the generation coming behind me." Coming from a person who is still very much in national and international demand, this is quite a statement. Apostle Barbara is at a point in her life when she could say she has given more than is even reasonable and that therefore she is going to slow down a little. No one would blame her or think less of her. But she has decided to do the opposite. She is an example of a true Samuel who is operating in the, "no competition zone."

The Bible says:

For where envy and self-seeking exist, confusion and every evil thing are there. (James 3:16, NKJV)

This is a season of building. We can't have confusion and evil sown into the midst of it. Both generations need to accept and honor the role and function that the other is to play. Those roles and functions shift and evolve over time, but the basis of honor does not. There are many Davids who want position before their time. They need to stay in the field and remain in the purifying fires of the Lord as their character is developed. David's lessons in the field are what prepared him for Goliath. If you leave the field too early, you move out of the timing of God. This is some of the confusion James mentions that is born of envy. Likewise, also, when the time comes

62

to anoint David as king, the Samuels must make room and space for this to happen and not withhold the oil. Samuel poured all he had, withholding nothing.

Some might feel that if they give all they have, they will have nothing left. They might feel that there has to be more purpose for their lives than merely anointing the next generation. Let me encourage you, there is. As with anything in the kingdom, when we give away, sow and plant, somehow multiplication occurs! When we help to fulfill others' callings, we fulfill our own. When we give away all we have, we come into increase and we end up full.

Arise, Samuels! Break out of every hindering structure and system! Refuse to bow to fear and hear the plan of God. Follow him on an awesome adventure and step into something that is totally new. You were called for such a time as this. Your contribution is vital and God does not want drop of your precious oil wasted, spilled or withheld. It has been stored up for divine purpose. Transform the orphan shepherds before you into kings.

In the next chapter, let's begin to dive into the lessons David needs to learn in the field. We will then move on to what I believe one of the biggest Goliaths this David generation is facing and how to face and conquer it. From there we will talk about David's tent, the place of Presence designed for encounter, and finally we will talk about becoming the bridge, building functional unity between the generations and working effectively together.

Chapter 6

KILL YOUR LION AND BEAR AND *THEN* WE'LL TALK...

Character Development for David

I was about twenty-one years old, serving in a ministry in upstate New York. We had just finished putting on a conference, which was not out of the ordinary for us; at the time we put on about ten per year. This conference had been a particularly glorious time in the presence of God. Then afterward we were blessed to have one of the speakers stay longer and address us personally. That person was none other than Mahesh Chavda. My friend and I affectionately call him, Master Yoda, a play on the Star Wars character who is the most powerful Jedi of them all. Always at peace, yet powerful and wise—that is Mahesh Chavda to a T.

There we were, listening and hanging on every word that Mahesh was speaking. (I have mentioned Mahesh and Bonnie a few times in this book already. If not are not familiar with them, I encourage you to look them up.) They are an amazing couple, and Mahesh has ministered around the world for over forty years. He has seen the most phenomenal, documented miracles you can possibly imagine. In his early days working with the late Derek Prince, Mahesh once saw the complete healing of a woman with no eyeballs in her eye sockets. The Lord actually formed totally new, blue eyes for her! Mahesh walks in a remarkable dimension of the glory of God.

We listened to story after story, delighting in every one, until Mahesh came to a more somber account. He started to encourage us as young people about our values and about being humble. Most of us listening to him were around the ages of eighteen to twenty-six. He spoke of being at a conference earlier that year that was filled with young people from all over the world. After he prayed, preached and poured out to these young people the entire weekend, he was on his way out when he was stopped by a young man in the hallway of the conference center. The young man told Mahesh how God had called him as a great apostle in his generation and how Mahesh would certainly be lucky to have a chance to pray for and impart to such an important person. As politely as he could, Mahesh declined and explained to the young person how he had to catch his flight and had to be on his way. The young person scoffed and went on his way.

Mahesh wasn't angry about the rudeness of this young man, and he certainly didn't dwell on the story. He simply used it as an example to encourage us to do better in our lives and to walk with God. He then moved on to another story and ended up the meeting by laying hands on all of us. I can't even begin to describe to you what I felt as he ministered to us. I had never before felt a weight and heaviness of the glory of God as I did that day. It changed me . . . as did the story of the young man he had encountered. Both became indelibly etched in my mind, although for totally different reasons.

Afterward I lay awake that night I thought a lot about the story he had told. I thought of it in the context of a past generation who understand respect, honor and due process in a way that the younger generation seems to have a hard time grasping. I felt so saddened at how far we in the younger generation seem to have fallen. I remembered how Joshua used to observe Moses and his encounters with the Lord, and how he had such a reverence for the glory that he would linger in the tent of meeting long after Moses had left. I recalled how Elisha poured water on the hands of Elijah, which was a job usually designated for a servant, as he served and honored the man of God. I thought about how Ruth clung to Naomi when all others had left her. She stayed and bound herself to her mother-in-law in faithfulness, sensing something in the older woman that she could not let go. I pictured how Jesus, our Lord himself, stooped down to wash the feet of his disciples in humility and love.

Mahesh's story has never left me and it has shaped and framed the context out of which I view things. I became concerned about the state of the younger generation and I considered my own blind spots and areas of weakness. I took encouragement from the stories about the lives of those men and women who have gone on before us, because they exemplify the values and heart of the kingdom.

As I stated in the previous chapter, I feel that there are some real lessons that the David generation needs to learn. We can't miss some lessons "in the field" before the anointing, lest we lack the foundation of character that will permit us to stand under the weight of the mantle. God wants to help us with this self-obsession that runs throughout the younger generation, this hyper-focus on personal achievement, accomplishment and self-worth. He wants to move us into a greater place of maturity and humility.

There is a process of God in the anointing. There was a long time from the pouring of the oil from Samuel onto David until he actually sat down on the throne. The "space between" was the most important for David. Even before he came before Goliath, he had already been trained on a lion and a bear.

> But David said to Saul, "Your servant has been keeping his father's sheep. When a lion or a bear came and carried off a sheep from the flock, I went after it, struck it and rescued the sheep from its mouth. When it turned on me, I seized it by its hair, struck it and killed it. Your servant has killed both the lion and the bear; this uncircumcised Philistine will be like one of them, because he has defied the armies of the living God. The LORD who rescued me from the paw of the lion and the paw of the bear will rescue me from the hand of this Philistine."

Saul said to David, "Go, and the LORD be with you."
(1 Samuel 17:34–37, NIV)

I believe in this David Generation that was born to kill giants. They've got the gall and the guts to do it, even in a time when it seems like no one else is stepping up to the plate. But they (we) have a lot to learn in the meantime as we prepare for some of our first great battles.

In other words, there are things that God wants to teach us in the *field of sheep* before we come to the *field of battle*. Let's look together at some of that.

Humility

Humility is a beautiful word, but what does it really mean? Many times people use it to mean a groveling, hunched-over person who thinks he or she is a pile of junk who cannot do anything. Does "humility" depict a kneeling, defeated, weak person who feels worthless? Humility can come in many forms, but it's not like that.

True humility is not a lack of confidence, identity or ability. It is something so much more than that. The Bible says:

Who is wise and understanding among you? Let them show it by their good life, by deeds done in the humility that comes from wisdom. (James 3:13, NIV)

If we are to bring the generations together, we need to have great wisdom on both sides. The Bible is clear on the fact that wisdom comes from humility (see Proverbs 15:33). Humility opens the door in our communications and actions for the wisdom of God to come forth.

There are a few words that are used to describe humility in the Bible. The first is *"tapeinophrosýnē."* This word is a noun, derived from *"tapeinós,"* which means, "low, humble" and *"phrén,"* which means "moderation as regulated by inner perspective." Besides "humility," the word means low, lowliness of human pride, a mindset of having a humble opinion of oneself, which is to say a deep sense of one's moral and intellectual littleness. Humility is an inside-out virtue produced by comparing ourselves to the Lord rather than to others. This brings our behavior into alignment with this inner revelation as it keeps us from being self-exalting, self-determining or self-inflated. For the believer, *"tapeinophrosýnē,"* humility, means living in complete dependence on the Lord, with no reliance on the self (i.e., "the flesh").

In other words, when we are humble, we are viewing ourselves and others from an *inner perspective* that allows us to regard ourselves and others from a place of complete reliance on the Lord, being fully aware of our inability, but also aware of *his ability.* Far from meaning that we believe we are worthless or nothing, we know that even in our humanity we are completely able to do what we are called to do through the One who empowers us.

We have to get this right. Usually we swing way too far one way or another, going from total self-degradation, weakness and self-hatred back to pride and a self-exalting opinion of ourselves.

With true humility, our inner perspective guides us well. When we are humble, in other words, completely reliant on the Lord, we are sensitive in a greater degree to the Holy Spirit. And the Holy Spirit will bring the generations together. The removal of our pride, insecurity and self-promotion will open lines of communication and foster unity—a unity that will turn the world upside-down.

I believe that it is this inner confidence that led David to the battle and gave him the courage to stand, fight and ultimately see the victory. There were some, though, who accused him of arrogance. To walk in true humility that is based in a healthy perspective, we will need to overcome the trap of judgment. This happens both within ourselves and as we experience it from others.

The Trap of Judgment

> *David asked the men standing near him, "What will be done for the man who kills this Philistine and removes this*

disgrace from Israel? Who is this uncircumcised Philistine
that he should defy the armies of the living God?"

They repeated to him what they had been saying and
told him, "This is what will be done for the man who kills
him."

When Eliab, David's oldest brother, heard him
speaking with the men, he burned with anger at him and
asked, "Why have you come down here? And with whom did
you leave those few sheep in the wilderness? I know how
conceited you are and how wicked your heart is; you came
down only to watch the battle." (1 Samuel 17:26–28, NIV)

David's inner confidence (humility) was formed in him when
he was alone with the Lord in the field. He had fought the lion and
the bear and had overcome them. He attributed these victories to the
Lord and not to his own strength. When it came to Goliath he knew
that God could and would deliver him from the hand of the Philistine
as well. But his brother burned with jealousy and anger. It caused
misunderstanding and a breach of communication and hindered them
from working together. It also released a judgment on David.

As I said above, we need humility, but we need God's
perspective on it. True humility is *empowering*. If we don't adopt the
right perspective on it, we will settle for a religious form of humility
that is totally void of any power.

In previous chapters, we talked about new paradigms and not
doing things the way they have always been done. There is a God-
given confidence in the younger generations that many, including
themselves, have misunderstood. Where did the opposition come
from when David wanted to stand up against Goliath? From his own
brother. A house divided cannot stand. As a younger generation, we
cannot fall into the trap of judgment and divisiveness. If we do, we
miss the birthright of our generation, which is to be giant-killers. We
were tailor-made to oppose Goliath, but misunderstanding and
judgment shuts down communication.

In that same passage of Scripture, after Eliab says what he
does, David's response is one of exasperation. He says in verse 29,

"can I not even speak?" and the Scripture says he then turned away from his brother. The end result was division and strife.

Not only did Eliab judge David, but Saul did as well. Neither of them could receive the package that their victory was coming in. They judged the outside appearance. Eliab judged a perceived heart motive of arrogance that was not accurate, and Saul judged the physical appearance of David. Saul told David point-blank that he couldn't beat Goliath:

> *Saul replied, "You are not able to go out against this Philistine and fight him; you are only a young man, and he has been a warrior from his youth."* (1 Samuel 17:33, NIV)

A wrong judgment can make a person lose all sense of true discernment. Eliab was jealous and accused David. We need true discernment and not wrong thinking, filtered through our sin and anger. We may see a seemingly arrogant young person before us where God sees a giant slayer who will bring victory to the masses! It is not our job to judge, only to guide. What may look like arrogance may actually be confidence born of relationship with God.

Every Monday night, I lead a prayer meeting at church. We often begin by praying or singing in the Spirit. We focus our intercession on different themes. That particular night, we were focused on physical healing for family members and people who were in the room. After the meeting, those we had prayed for began to share how they were feeling.

One person shared about a need that had not yet been healed. Immediately, a young man whom I had only met a few times offered to pray for this person. He shared how he had been on a missions trip and had seen God heal the very need that was being described. I have to be honest; I immediately started to judge him. I thought, "I don't even know this kid. He isn't even a member of my church. Who does he think he is to pray for someone?" The Holy Spirit quickly caught me and I could see the Eliab in my own heart. This young man was full of passion for healing and he had faith because he'd had an encounter with God! Why would I be opposed to that?

I'm not saying you must let anyone do anything, but neither should you hinder the godly zeal of a young person. I was moving in judgment and mistaking godly confidence for arrogance.

Eliab judged and accused. Saul tried to put his armor on David. Meanwhile David was already robed in the glory of God, which gave him the inner perspective of victory and confidence! He was walking in humility *that was empowering.* David couldn't be bound to the old structures. He was called to pioneer a whole new generation of warriors.

Davids, let's get this right!

Honor

God is so good to us in his development of us. He takes us through seasons of learning and we emerge victorious in what he worked in us. But then we go through another level of learning to achieve a higher revelation. I have found that this pattern holds true in life no matter what age you are or where you are. There is a process in God.

God taught David many things in the shepherds' field. He emerged from those lessons and overcame the champion Goliath. After a season of victory however, David again found himself in the fields of learning. This time, one of the main lessons he was learning was honor.

As I said in the previous chapter, it didn't take long for Saul to become insanely jealous over David. Every dealing Saul had with David from that time on became deceptive. Saul even gave his daughter in marriage to David with a hidden motive of David's harm (see 1 Samuel 18:21).

In the transition season, David had to navigate very carefully. Remember, he was anointed to be king, but Saul still held the position for many years. In those years, *in the midst of persecution,* David learned honor. It was one of the most important lessons he was to learn, and likewise it is for this David generation.

71

Early on, David had to flee for his very life:

Now the distressing spirit from the LORD came upon Saul as he sat in his house with his spear in his hand. And David was playing music with his hand. Then Saul sought to pin David to the wall with the spear, but he slipped away from Saul's presence; and he drove the spear into the wall. So David fled and escaped that night. (1 Samuel 19:9–10, NKJV)

This was the beginning of several times that David had to flee, move and hide from Saul as Saul tried to kill him. I am sure you know this, but life isn't fair sometimes! What was happening to David wasn't fair, but even in the midst of it God was working for David's good. It may seem crazy, but God will use an unrighteous structure and leader at times to teach you kingdom truths you could not learn otherwise. For a fact, the person you are in the midst of that structure is who you will be on the other side of it. How you sow honor—even to unrighteous leaders—is closely linked to how you will lead when you have achieved a position.

I love a line from the 1993 movie, *Cool Runnings*. There is a scene in the movie where Derice, one of the main characters, is asking his coach about Olympic gold medals. The coach had actually cheated in the Olympics he competed in even after he received several gold medals. Derice cannot understand why someone would cheat even after achieving such an amazing thing. The coach (played by the late John Candy) turns to Derice and says, "If you are not enough without it, you will never be enough with it."

I want to say something to all the Davids reading this who feel they are being kept unjustly under a Saul structure. First, you need to have the humility to realize that what feels like a Saul structure is actually the process of God you are in. The process is not meant to destroy you, but rather to build your character and to actually qualify you to lead. Secondly, if you are indeed under a Saul structure, choose the path of honor. If you cannot honor *without the crown*, you will never be a leader of honor *with the crown*.

God gave David opportunities to honor Saul even in the midst of Saul's insanity and unrighteousness. We looked at this in the previous chapter on the Saul structure, but we need to look at it again through the lens of honor. In the previous chapter we took the perspective of allowing God to deal with Saul, here I want us to see the heart of David:

> *Then the men of David said to him, "This is the day of which the LORD said to you, 'Behold, I will deliver your enemy into your hand, that you may do to him as it seems good to you.'" And David arose and secretly cut off a corner of Saul's robe. Now it happened afterward that David's heart troubled him because he had cut Saul's robe. And he said to his men, "The LORD forbid that I should do this thing to my master, the LORD's anointed, to stretch out my hand against him, seeing he is the anointed of the LORD." (1 Samuel 24:4, NKJV)*

David *honored the anointing above the leader*. We have got to understand that leaders are fallible, but God clothes weak humanity in his anointing. The anointing accomplishes what it is meant to do because God sees to it that this happens! However, the flesh is still there, and will always be there, in every single leader ever to walk the earth. David honored the anointing on Saul and therefore *he honored God*.

We honor God in everything. The basis of all honor for one another is a heart posture of honor toward God. Some would say, "I honor God, not man." I want to challenge that sentiment by saying that to honor God, you have to honor man! There are limits, of course, but it is something this David generation has to learn.

Through the persecution and pain, David's heart toward Saul remained godly. In another passage, we read:

> *Then Abishai said to David, "God has delivered your enemy into your hand this day. Now therefore, please, let me strike him at once with the spear, right to the earth; and I will not have to strike him a second time!"*

But David said to Abishai, "Do not destroy him; for who can stretch out his hand against the LORD's anointed, and be guiltless?" David said furthermore, "As the LORD lives, the LORD shall strike him, or his day shall come to die, or he shall go out to battle and perish. The LORD forbid that I should stretch out my hand against the LORD's anointed.
(1 Samuel 26: 8–11, NKJV)

David again had the opportunity to kill Saul, but chose to obey the Lord and honor him. He looked to the Lord for his vindication and stayed *in the fire* of the dealings of God. He did not move out of time, but trusted and yielded to God to do for him what he said he would.

In the next chapter, let's look at some real giants that this David is facing; specifically, the giant of sexual sin. I am including this because I feel it is vital for Samuels to be aware of the enormity of this challenge. Sexual sin is a modern-day Goliath that wants to kill this David generation and enslave them. Not only do the Samuels need to be aware, but they need to know what to do in terms of strategic action and intervention to rescue David. We will look at that a little bit in chapter 7 and specifically the role of Samuel in chapter 8 entitled, "Hope Solutions."

Chapter 7

THE CALL OF SEDUCTION

A Giant That Stands in Our Way...

Of all of the things that David struggled through and learned from, the seduction of Bathsheba is unforgettable, from the moment he saw her bathing on her rooftop until he ended face-down on the floor pleading for the life of his son. What began as lust and covetousness ended in betrayal, murder and death. David was almost defeated by something that looked a whole lot less intimidating and formidable than Goliath, but that underneath was actually far more dangerous than the boastful giant.

This Goliath of seduction is one of the chief foes this younger generation faces. To call it simply "lust" seems like a gross understatement anymore. In many ways, what we are facing is a perversion of all healthy sexual identity and interaction. The statistics are staggering and alarming and the age at which young people are exposed to pornography is getting younger and younger. I will share some of those statistics in a moment, but let me start with a personal note.

As an individual, I have struggled with lust. I put it out there plain to see for a number of reasons, one of the chief being that I strongly feel that the only way we are going to make any headway on this issue is by leaders being totally vulnerable and honest. We have somehow built a culture of fear and shame around this issue in the Body of Christ, and this shame hinders the light of God from shining on and exposing the darkness and lies. It's almost like one of the United States Army's famous policies, "don't ask, don't tell." We don't want to ask one another or tell one another because of the level of shame and fear of rejection that are associated with the issue.

Growing up as a millennial, sexual images and pornography were readily available on TV and in my teenage years even on "dial up" Internet. It was late into my teens before I was exposed to porn by a friend, but from that point on, it burned into my brain like a constant, gnawing force trying to consume my entire thought life. I remember that every time I would look at something sinful, I would lock myself in the bathroom and cry, look myself in the mirror, tell myself how much I hated myself, repent (or at least I thought it was repentance) and swear up and down I would never do it again. That cycle and pattern repeated itself for years and years. Eventually shame turns into numbness and you stop even believing yourself that you can be truly free. That numbness turns into a coldness that pries you away from God as the lie begins to set in: "God doesn't want a hypocrite like you."

If you have a negative message like that in your mind every time you approach God, chances are that somewhere along the way you are going to stop even trying to approach him. Who likes to feel bad about himself or hopeless about a situation over and over and over again? No one. It wasn't until I had a dramatic open vision in which I encountered the love of the Father as an ocean of liquid love that I began to see the light at the end of the tunnel. God led me on a journey out of shame and fear and into the confidence of being an heir of Christ and a son of God.

I share this to bring hope and perhaps some level of confidence to those who will read this book who struggle with this same issue. There is a way of escape. Love has a name and a voice. Love is waiting and longing to rescue you from your cage of self-hatred. I also share it to establish the compassion I have for those who struggle with this issue. I am not going to pontificate on and on about righteousness and holiness. I hope to stir you up to believe in something (Someone) more and for you to join the great battle of the ages as a good soldier. Time to get in line, David generation!

If the David generation is to fulfill its purpose, we must see deliverance in this area. In addition, Samuels must become aware of the magnitude of the problem so that they can intervene. It has grown very quickly from something that seemed to be on the back burner of the consciousness of the Church to a front and center focus. We need a wholesale revolution in this area so that a generation can rise up with a new slogan: "Not even a hint!" (Taken from Ephesians 5:3, which reads, *"Among you there must not be even a hint of sexual immorality, or of any kind of impurity, or of greed, because these are improper for God's holy people."*)

The Cold, Hard Facts

I want to draw your attention to some statistics concerning this matter from a study that Joshua McDowell commissioned. He has stood by his statistics and information for over fifty years and so I feel I can quote him with a great degree of confidence.

McDowell stated that he believes Internet pornography to be the greatest encumbrance of the Church in its entire history. To begin with, he points to the size of the porn industry.

In 1998, there were 14 million Internet pornography sites. That statistic has jumped every year exponentially. In 2003, there were 260 million; in 2006, 420 million; in 2010, 500 million; in 2012, 800 million and by the time he gave his lecture in early 2015 he stated that there were over 1.79 billion Internet pornography sites worldwide. If one person spent two minutes on each of those sites, it would take that person 4,083,000 days to look at them all which would equate to 11,180 years! He went on to state that of all Internet searches worldwide, one quarter (25 percent) are searches for porn, 35 percent of all downloads worldwide are porn and 30 percent of *all Internet activity worldwide* is porn.

Of all pornography users, 68 percent are twenty-five years old and younger. Of that percentage, 78 percent are twelve to twenty-five years old. Ninety percent of all eight to sixteen-year-old boys have viewed porn and the largest consumers of Internet porn, according to that industry, are between the ages of twelve and seventeen. In its data analysis of those who are consumers of their "product," the pornography industry claims that 30 percent are children—not young adults or teenagers, but *children*. The U.S. Department of Education reports that 67 percent of all three to nine-year-olds are active online and 35 percent of those children visit porn sites. The current average age to be exposed to pornography is eight years old.

When I first read these statistics I thought, *these must be "nonbeliever" statistics.* Unfortunately, that is not the case. Even among pastors and leaders this is not the case. Statistically speaking there are only a few percentage points between believers and nonbelievers. Again, according to the statistics that Joshua McDowell presented, 77 percent of evangelical men view porn, 54 percent of pastors view porn and 80–90 percent of youth pastors watch pornography!

At first the statistics are hard to believe, but the deeper you delve into the hard data, as McDowell has, the more blaringly clear the facts become. Pornography is an epidemic of gigantic proportions, towering over the younger generations like Goliath, seeking to kill and enslave them before they even begin.

What can we possibly do? Can we even win this battle? I believe that the answer is Yes, even though the odds are against us. God is still a God of miracles and the good news is that we will not be fighting on our own. I believe all of heaven is about to intervene in this and that the Samuels are a huge part of that. God's desire is for a glorious Church to bring in a great harvest of souls. Many have prophesied about this as I shared in the first chapter. I believe that even now there are divine strategies coming forth which are going to turn the tables on the plan of the enemy.

I want to look together at a few the Lord has showed me. To say the least, this is not an exhaustive synopsis, but it's a small contribution which I hope will start an avalanche of momentum in those reading this.

Something Greater

Dietrich Bonhoeffer wrote, "The pursuit of purity is not about the suppression of lust, but about the reorientation of one's life to a larger goal." This is such an incredible statement. Bonhoeffer is saying, in essence, "There is more!" Punitive religious rhetoric does not work. In fact, drives the issue home too intensely. When you hold out something like a medicine and say it is a cure, it had better work! If it doesn't the person won't believe what you are saying next time. We have held out discipline and formulas and structures and more to this generation and none of them have worked. I am not saying the word of God changes, or that there is not merit in those things. What I am saying is that somehow in our declaration of the truth, we have not revealed a *greater glory* to them, which would capture their attention and affection.

The Lord spoke to me several years ago and asked me a question. He said, "Why do you like to watch movies and identify with the characters who are sacrificing to perform amazing feats that defy the odds, but are unwilling to live that way?" Wow! It certainly caused me to pause and think. One of the things that came out in my dialogue with the Lord over that question was that I felt I had no opportunity and no one to lead me. He spoke to me so softly, but yet with a power that turned my life around, saying, "Son, follow me and I will lead you into the epic journey of the ages . . . and you will have a part to play." It turned out his question to me wasn't meant to put me down and demotivate me, but it was a divine invitation.

This divine invitation can turn this entire issue around. There is not only *something* greater to live for, but *someone* greater. That Someone can fill the longings, needs and desires that pornography tries to satisfy. When you taste of the true glory of the Lord, you can't go back to the counterfeit.

It's like being able to identify counterfeit money. Part of the training for people who work with large amounts of currency is exposure. People are exposed to real currency over and over again. They become so accustomed to the real thing that when they see the fake, they can identify it immediately.

But that's not what we are doing. It's almost as if our strategy for the younger generation has been to tell them and show them over and again what the fake is: "Watch out for this! Be aware of this! Don't do this!" And all the while the real is left out of the equation. Because they don't know the real, the counterfeit can slip in and start to take hold in the economy of their hearts. It may look real, sound real and feel real, but there is no value to what is fake and fabricated.

We have fabricated relationships, battles and realities. We created entire worlds that give a sense of stimulation and purpose, but leave us so empty. Countless cultures and subcultures have been created. Where is the culture of the Glory? Where are the young, hungry Davids who are so captivated by heaven's reality that they hang out just to talk about it? Where are the ones who share the heart of David and say, "One thing have I desired!"

I want to point out one of these subcultures, the "gamers." You see accounts of gamers who get completely immersed in playing a game that they refuse to eat or go to the bathroom or even move at all. Some of these gamers have actually died as they stared into their reality, their fabricated world. For example, on March 3, 2015, I read an account about a twenty-four-year-old man who died after a nineteen-hour gaming marathon. The autopsy report stated that he was so completely dehydrated and malnourished after gaming for nineteen hours straight that his body had simply shut down; it could no longer function.

In another account, I read about a twenty-two-year-old man in Taiwan whose father had told him to stop playing video games. He was so angry and distraught that he set himself on fire and burned to death. His parents and police found him in the morning.

He was just getting ready to graduate from his studies and was said to have been stressed out about finding a job after graduating.

These stories are just a couple examples of the desperation of this generation. It's almost as if the part of our minds and spirits that are meant to encounter God and access the revelatory realm of dreams and visions has been overtaken by these other things. The part of the brain that was meant to access God has grown bored and disinterested because it has been fed the counterfeit over and again. I am not saying that games and movies are bad; all I am saying is that they are subpar compared to what God can supply. Two things cannot occupy the same space. We have generations alive today that are desperate, bored and longing for something more. They are dissatisfied because they feel that they have seen everything. When the new technology or movie or game comes out, they flock to it . . . but only for a time, until that becomes disinteresting as well. The need for something more and better, more interactive and engaging, is constant; it is never completely satisfied.

In the midst of all of this, I am actually encouraged! I know that God is getting ready to release such a divine revelation of himself over this generation that it will leave them totally satisfied. They may feel like they have seen everything, but in actual fact they *haven't seen anything yet*. A light shines in the darkness with a hope that cannot be surpassed. I see a redemptive quality within this David generation that God will use to turn them into revolutionaries.

This David generation is a prophetic generation. That is why they crave these games and movies and virtual realities! They are hungry for vision, for the supernatural and for the epic. When God shows them who he is, a divine exchange will occur; addiction to what the world has to offer will be traded for what God can and will offer them—visions of himself. He will leave them speechless and breathless. He will invite them into the most amazing story of all time! He will show them that they have a part to play in this mighty revival that will sweep the earth and bring about the culmination of the ages. We are progressively moving toward a revelation of Jesus Christ. Every knee will bow in awesome agony before the One whom they have (either knowingly or unknowingly) longed for their entire life.

The bigger picture will come. That longing to be a part of something greater than one's own life to which Bonhoeffer referred will be revealed in a glorious way to the younger generation. God will remove the thin veil of their pale reality and invite them into his living dimension of inexpressible, unapproachable light and love! I want to tell you, once they experience that, they will never go back to the counterfeit or the subpar. They will *run* into their calling, destiny and purpose. They will give everything!

Can you imagine the devotion that it takes to sit down in front of a game for hours on end in order to master every nuance, move and strategy of that game? It takes hours and hours of time and dedication, and it requires prioritizing that game over all else, even sleep. Sometimes the things we criticize in this generation are actually those things which are intrinsically born into them by God. That devotion, dedication and persistence is simply misdirected. God will use it mightily for his glory. It is a gift, currently raw and misguided.

We need to speak hope and life to the younger generations. In parody after parody, they are referred to as Millennials and Generation X, and while some of the parodies are pretty funny, the message behind them is very derogatory. It says, "You are lazy. You will never amount to anything. You are arrogant. You're a whiner and complainer." I am not saying there is not some truth in these accusations. We can see many issues in these generations, but likewise there were lots of issues in other generations.

The Baby Boomers ushered in the sexual revolution of the 1960s, which resulted in cataclysmic societal repercussions that pounded away at an already degrading moral fiber. The generations before them had tolerated racism and gross injustices in a very different America than we have now. These are not indictments. What I am trying to say is that every generation has their sinful issues. But thanks be to God who is faithful to visit every single generation with a move of his Spirit! That is what we need to be talking about, praying for and focusing on. We need to speak hope and life to the younger generations and call forth their redemptive destiny. They can and will fulfill their purpose.

There is a scene from a movie called *Kung Fu Panda*. (I know—another movie reference. I am a Millennial, after all!) Some of you may know the story. It's a Kung Fu movie about a character who, against all odds, fulfils his destiny and brings peace in the midst of a threat of violence. The old Kung Fu master named Shifu who is played by Dustin Hoffman had a student who had turned against him. He brought destruction to the city and could only be stopped by a turtle named Oogway, who in the story is the originator of Kung Fu. They put the wayward student in prison, but one day Oogway has a vision that he will escape.

Dustin Hoffman's character Shifu is filled with fear at these words. He asks Oogway how this enemy can be stopped and Oogway reminds him of the ancient prophecy of the Dragon Warrior. They set out to find this dragon warrior who ends up being a big, slow panda. Shifu is furious. He had been working with five students for many years. He had thought that one of them would end up being the Dragon Warrior and is very distraught when the panda is chosen. He'd had a picture in his mind of who this great warrior would be. In his anger he goes outside to a peach tree where he finds Oogway. He expresses his frustration to Oogway about how he doesn't believe that the big, slow panda can defeat the enemy. Their dialogue is so simple, but so powerful:

Oogway: My friend, the panda will never fulfill his destiny, nor you yours, until you let go of the illusion of control.
Shifu: Illusion?
Oogway: Yes.
[*points at peach tree*]
Oogway: Look at this tree, Shifu. I cannot make it blossom when it suits me, nor make it bear fruit before its time.
Shifu: But there are things we *can* control.
[*kicks the tree so that peaches fall*]
Shifu: I can control when the fruit will fall!
[*he slices a peach and throws the pit to the ground*]

Shifu: I can control where to plant the seed! That is no illusion, Master!

Oogway: Ah, yes. But no matter what you do, that seed will grow to be a peach tree. You may wish for an apple or an orange, but you will get a peach.

Shifu: But a peach cannot defeat Tai Lung!

Oogway: [*folding dirt over the peach pit*] Maybe it *can*, if you are willing to guide it, to nurture it. To believe in it.

Maybe we wish that these younger generations were apples or oranges rather than what they are. Perhaps we think that they are poorly equipped to defeat the threatening giants of their time. No matter what we may wish, they are who they are . . . and God made them this way.

Rather than trying to change them and make them fit an impossible mold, why don't we work with what we have? God knows what he is doing. The generation alive now is able to fulfill his purpose for their lives and defeat every enemy. This includes this Goliath of seduction that manifests itself in so many different ways. Let's not confuse immaturity and need for growth for a total absence of ability. The seed may be small and fragile, immature and weak, but from that seed will grow greatness.

Will we guide it, nurture it, believe in it? If we will, the sky is the limit.

Chapter 8

HOPE SOLUTIONS

Encounter the Master of Breakthroughs

Take a deep breath…Whew! You made it through that last chapter! Good job! I know that was intense and a lot to absorb. As I was researching all of the information so many mixed emotions came up in me. I started with disbelief and fought through anger and then even had to combat despair. The situation seems to be overwhelming, but I don't believe that we are without hope. God is the God of the miraculous. I believe that even now as you read this, there are countless thousands whom the Holy Spirit is moving upon who will give themselves fully to the Lord Jesus in purity. There is a Remnant. That word, "remnant" is not a word that is often used in normal conversation, but it is so appropriate for what God is doing right now.

God has always moved through a remnant people. All throughout the Bible and all throughout history, it was never the majority that did great things for God, but rather the *minority*. Esther went alone before the king although she knew it could cost her life. Jeremiah prophesied the word of the Lord even when all the other prophets were saying exactly the opposite. Jesus went alone to the cross when those around him abandoned and forsook him. God doesn't need a lot of people to obey him to accomplish his desire; he just needs *a few courageous ones.*

In the previous chapter I laid out some of the issues and challenges that stand before us. We also delved a little into some redemptive strategies. In this chapter, I want to speak to the hope of what is to come. We are not going to be defeated. God will have a victorious Bride without spot or wrinkle before he comes. He is not going to leave us in this mess. He has always and will always be there, in our corner, fighting our battles with us and we can partner together with him.

"Therefore, since all these things will be dissolved, what manner of persons ought you to be in holy conduct and godliness?" (2 Peter 3:11, NKJV). This passage speaks to us about living. setting forth a question from the context of what preceded the verse. In paraphrase, it asks "In light of this, what is your response?" I feel that way as I pray through the issues at hand. What are we to do? Are we to bury our heads in the sand and hope that this all goes away? Are we to live bitter, angry suspicious lives, afraid of getting close to anyone who may be infected with this disease of lust? No, God has called us to live; and live abundantly. There are answers to these questions and solutions to the problems.

A friend once told me that there is a key to every lock. No matter how impenetrable a safe may be or how elaborate the security measures, there is a key to every locked-up, hidden and guarded place. Nothing is beyond breaking through. The good news for us is that according to 2 Samuel 5:20, God is the master of breakthroughs! I love this verse: *"David went to Baal Perazim, and David defeated them there; and he said, 'The Lord has broken through my enemies before me, like a breakthrough of water.'"* David had just defeated the Philistines, but prior to that, he had accomplished something awesome; something that had never been done before. As the generations come together, we will accomplish what has never been done before.

The one people who were not driven off when Joshua cleared out the Promised Land were the Jebusites. According to Joshua 15:63 it said that the Jebusites, an enemy of Israel, could not be driven out by Judah and lived with them there to, "this day" (when that part of Scripture was written). Then, as we read in 2 Samuel 5, David finished the work of prior generations by climbing into the city through the sewer pipe and making his way into the enemy kingdom to gain victory. David and his men came through a "water shaft," according to the New King James version of verse 8. Water shafts or water drains were used as sewer pipes to transport human waste out of the dwellings and public places. In large cities in that time there was little to no sanitation and water shafts helped to maintain some degree of cleanliness. In other words, David and his men crawled through a very dirty place, one which was used for transporting filth, so that they could come into a place of victory and conquer the city. It was a momentous victory and occasion not only for David, but for the whole nation of Israel.

The Jebusites were a pagan tribe of Canaan, the ancient people whom the Israelites were commanded drive out of the Promised Land. They practiced all kinds of evil including divination and occult practices which included human sacrifice. They were a formidable foe and they mocked, insulted and defeated the people of Israel time and again. In fact, when David came up to besiege them, they even mocked him and said that the blind and lame of their people could ward him off (see 2 Samuel 5:6). But David humbled himself in a sense and came into their city through a way that they did not expect. He found the key to the locked-up and impenetrable fortress!

Just as the enemies of lust and seduction seem to be impenetrable, like a fortress of iniquity that mocks us, there is a key to bringing them down. As you read this, I want you to envision yourself like David, coming through the murky, dirty places that are like a confined, dirty, nasty tunnel of sin. But as a David generation, you will emerge from that confined, locked-up place with sword in hand. You are the ones who have been anointed by your Samuels and empowered by love. You will rout out an unsuspecting, arrogant, age-old enemy because God will give you the victory.

Let's look together at some keys that will be able to unlock this fortress of seduction.

Eyes to See

Have you ever heard of a linchpin? A linchpin is a fastener used to prevent a wheel from sliding off its axle. Sometimes, the word is used figuratively to mean something (or someone) that holds together the parts of a complex structure.

Linchpins are small, but they are capable of holding together large, complicated structures. When we look at this Goliath of pornography and perversion in our generation, it is a complicated weblike structure of the Enemy. However, it is all held together by the Enemy's linchpins of deceit and lies. The Enemy spins things together like a spider web, but if you pull the right strands (linchpins) of the web, the whole thing immediately falls apart. In this battle, God is showing us the linchpins so that we can unravel the web of the Enemy. I want to refer to these keys as "hope solutions." Let's explore them together.

Fathers and Mothers

One of the main linchpins holding together this structure of iniquity is lies about the fathers and mothers of the Samuel generation. This is a giant, not unlike the Goliath that stared David down and hurled insults and contempt upon him. This seductive spirit that has captured this generation in its snare is a formidable foe, one that this David generation cannot face alone. Godly fathers and mothers are vitally needed, and there are some challenges.

Significant challenges come from the fact that this is not just a single-generation issue. It has captured much of the Church and most of the generational demographics across the board. Therefore, as we begin to look at bringing freedom and health to the David generation, we must first address the freedom and health of those who seek to help them. As Jesus said, *"can the blind lead the blind? Will they not both fall into a pit?"* (Luke 6:39, NIV). If the Samuel generation is going to help free the David generation from this mocking, menacing Goliath that seeks to destroy them, they first have to be free themselves.

I know many in the older generation, those who should be fathers and mothers, who are still caught as children in the basic truths of the Word. They have not been able to come to a place of maturity or healing themselves in this issue and so in some cases, they do not have authority or clarity. In spite of this, they are so desperately needed. The David generation is longing and looking for fathers and mothers to help to lead them out of bondage, men and women who have slain their own Goliaths of lust and can show them the way to victory.

Jesus said, *"If Satan casts out Satan, he is divided against himself. How then will his kingdom stand?"* (Matthew 12:26, NKJV). We need fathers and mothers who will stand up and do what is necessary to overcome and conquer this issue in their own lives, those who will pay the price and do everything in their power to draw the line and say, "this far and no farther." Given the level of saturation and bombardment of this spirit in our culture and society, that it is not going to be easy. It is going to take fasting, prayer, determination and accountability in large amounts in order to see the full victory. Although it will not be easy, a remnant of warriors will give themselves fully to the fight and will press through to victory.

I am in no way saying that all of the pressure rests on the shoulders of the Samuel generation in regard to this issue. The David generation is going to have to make a decision to face off with the Goliath of seduction on their own before they will see God use their weak "five stones" to bring it down. They have their own choices and decisions to make. What I am saying however, is that the call comes to the fathers and the mothers to stand and fight with them. If the fathers and mothers will fight and not retreat, the younger generation will come behind them.

The fathers and mothers are called to clear the way. If they don't, God will still make a way just as when David went against Goliath, but that generation will not come all the way into the call that God has for them. No one went with David as he faced off against the incredibly large and powerful giant, Goliath. His brothers judged and mocked him, and the rest of the army cowered in fear, as did their king. God helped David on that day and he got the glory. God will always make a way, but I feel that it is in his heart to see a unified fight across the generations over this issue. God wants everyone to stand up and say, "enough!" He desires to see a synergy among the generations, not failure, disappointment and division.

Moses failed to go into the Promised Land. Joshua failed to drive out the Jebusites. David had blood on his hands and so could not build the Temple. In each one of these situations, there was something that the older generation left behind for the next one coming after them to handle. With each generation's failure to fully accomplish what God had called them to, it became a bit harder for the next generation coming behind. What would happen if the generations all worked together in a common purpose to kill this giant? I believe that there would be a great victory!

Overcoming the Religious Structure

One of the other challenges we need to understand is what I refer to as "the religious spirit." The religious spirit is a structure of fear and judgment based on self-righteousness that seeks to control and manipulate. It is the structure that opposes every major move of God.

There is so much fear in the David generation when it comes to confessing what they are struggling with. Some might have taken a chance once or twice along the way to come clean and bring their struggle out into the open only to be met with judgment, legalism and shame.

There is so much confusion in the David generations when it comes to sexuality. As I mentioned in the statistics in the last chapter, the average age to be exposed to pornography is eight years old. Can you imagine what kind of warping of the mind that even five years of exposure to perverted images of unhealthy sexuality can do to someone? If the average age of exposure is eight, then after five years that young person would be a thirteen-year-old coming into puberty and physical maturity already having a developed interpretation of what sex is. That interpretation in many cases has come from the Internet. It will be twisted, warped and confusing. If they seek help from a pastor, leader or parent and experience either actual or perceived rejection it will send them down a path of isolation and further dysfunction.

We have to realize that someone is going to educate our children on human sexuality. Who do we want that to be? Do we want it to be the public schools? The young friend who is struggling with the same things, only maybe worse? Do we want it to be Google? The school of thought that says, "This will just go away over time" is completely unrealistic.

There is an account of a twenty-five-year-old teacher in a North Carolina school teaching her third grade class by reading from a book called, *King and King*. The book is a tale about two kings who loved each other and it culminates with a kiss between the two of them. It's hard to imagine the level of confusion that this produces in the children who hear the story. What happens to their questions, their confusion? Does it get bottled up? What direction does it moves in? Where is it met? As of 2009 there were 20,000 copies of this book in print. That may not seem like a lot, but it represents a lot of young minds being affected and confused.

Fathers and mothers, grandparents and grandmothers, Sunday school teachers, pastors, this issue is not going to go away. It has to be addressed and talked about. Joshua McDowell said he started talking to his children as young as possible about sex. Why? Because he wanted to be the one to frame their context. Are we willing to delve into the sewer with this David generation in order to see victory? Are we willing to become the hope solutions we are praying for?

Creating a Judgment-Free Zone

A gym business called Planet Fitness that has gained a lot of clientele over the past few years. They don't cater to the overly "buff" or "in shape" people; in fact, they invite people who are at a nominal level of fitness. Their famous phrase is Judgment Free Zone. It has actually gained them a lot of credibility in the general public's mind because people feel that anyone can go there, participate and get healthy. They are not being met with judgment, but rather with encouragement. Planet Fitness has created an environment in which you can take a risk, even look silly, as you achieve your fitness goal.

Sometimes the secular world can get it so right and we as the Church can get it so wrong! Many more elite gyms are being put out of business by this chain that started very small, but is now a giant franchise. They worked from the premise that the general public in America was *not healthy*. Many times in the Church, we expect people to come in and be healthy right out of the gate when in fact, it is unrealistic to think that way. Looking back at the statistics I put into the previous chapter; we are obviously not working with a population either inside or outside of the Church that is healthy. People are unhealthy and they need nutrition and a change of lifestyle that will provide an environment of growth.

We have got to create a judgment-free zone in the Church! We need to start celebrating risk-takers and those who allow themselves to be vulnerable instead of becoming uncomfortable around such people or ostracizing them. Those in leadership must create an atmosphere of love and acceptance. No question should be "off the table." No question or comment should evoke a sense of shock. Given the level of perversion in what the average person is seeing we have got to be prepared for questions about same-sex sexuality, oral sex, masturbation, etc. People have seen it all, and chances are they have an embedded memory of it, whether they want to or not.

From a scientific perspective, when someone sees something, chemicals such as norepinephrine are released in the brain that help imprint the image onto the person's mind and neurological pathways. In adults, images are "written" on the brain and new neurological pathways are created in as little as twenty seconds. The younger the individual is, the faster this can happen, even in as little as one second! We desperately need the Holy Spirit to rewrite our brains and cleanse us from iniquity. His love opens the doors to freedom.

Leo Tolstoy said, "Everyone thinks of changing the world, but no one thinks of changing himself." I believe that we have to start to become the change that we want to see. We have to create this atmosphere of *empathy, love, acceptance* and *hope for freedom.* We must have clear sight, which can only happen when we are love-driven and not judgment-driven. It is going to take both generations to bring down this Goliath, both fully committed to one another and to the process. Ask yourself, "What am I willing to do to become the answer to my own prayers?" If each of us will answer that and act upon it with true love that reaches the heart, we will win the victory.

Destiny Beckons

We have gone through a progression in this book. First we set the stage for the move that God is bringing forth. Then we called forth the Samuels and differentiated them from the Sauls and the Saul structure. We reviewed the "lion and bear lessons" that David has to go through and learn from and we have looked at some towering Goliaths. But we cannot stop here. We have to see this David generation fulfill its destiny with the help and partnership of the Samuels. There is a purpose for the oil and it's not just to learn, wander in the desert and contend with enemies and giants. The purpose of the oil is to rule and reign! That ruling and reigning has to be from a place of "one thing" (see Psalm 27:4).

In the next chapters, I want to look at the Tabernacle of David; the tent of God's Presence. This was the place where David's rule and reign was strengthened and it is a key to this generation fulfilling its destiny. I want to look at the role the Tabernacle of David must play in the unfolding of what God is doing and the "ruling and reigning" mindset. Next, I want to look at the heart of "one thing." Then finally, let's look at some things the David generation needs to understand and add to the Tabernacle of David movement if it is to hit the mark with precision.

Chapter 9

DAVID'S TENT

An Apostolic People Who Rule

I will never forget the first time I was in Israel in 2006. I was in awe of the culture, the people, the land and the beauty. It was as though I had stepped into the very manifestation of the faithfulness of a God who keeps his word. It was an experience that shaped my life, but there was one particular experience that has been etched on my mind and heart.

One of the evenings in the midst of a very busy tour, we had free time, and I wandered down the streets of Jerusalem. I walked through busy little street corners, past quiet bistros with musicians playing on the guitar or violin, captured by art all around me. But then I began to hear a sound that was literally shaking the rocks at my feet as I got closer and closer. It was a tribal sound, an ancient sound, yet one that echoed and pulsed with the strength and vigor of youth. I was immensely curious and started to make my way as fast as I could toward that sound.

The closer I got, the more obvious it began to be what I was hearing. It was a crowd of youth at least 150 strong clustered together in the city square on Ben Yehuda street, one of the main strips that runs through the center of Jerusalem. They were singing and dancing in unison as they shouted together the words of a melody that shook me to my core. The words that they kept saying were, "Moshiach!" and "Sheyavo!" They kept saying them over and over as they clapped and danced and stomped their feet in unison.

94

They were as one voice and their cry echoed throughout the night sky. It seemed to shake the very heavens and the earth.

I asked one of the people who was standing there what they were saying. The man smiled at me and asked me a few questions such as, "where are you from?" before he actually answered my question. I think it gave him a certain level of satisfaction that someone who was so clearly an outsider was so interested in a language and cultural experience. He smiled again at me and said, "They are declaring that the messiah will come in their time. "Moshiach" means "Anointed One" and "Sheyavo" means, "He will come!"

This statement went through me like a lightning bolt. In that moment I felt the Lord speak to me, "There is a generation alive on the earth right now that will raise such a cry that it will prepare the way for my coming. They are a prophetic generation, a David generation, heralding a cry that shakes heaven and earth!" I thanked the person and turned to leave. As I was wandering back, finding my way through the winding streets, I began to ask the Lord what the key was for this prophetic generation. I felt him speak to my heart one phrase: "the Tabernacle of David."

This was a phrase that I was very familiar with. At the time I had been with a ministry called Eagles' Wings led by Dr. Robert Stearns for four years. The Tabernacle of David was one of the key themes that God had revealed to Robert. It held a special meaning and significance to me and I began to be moved deeply in my journey back through those stone streets late at night. This is an experience that I have held in my heart for many years; ten years later it still is as riveting to me as the first moment I heard the sound. Those young Jewish people shook the ground and forever burned that sound into my spirit.

This Is That Day

One of Robert Stearns' favorite phrases was from Amos 9:11: *"In that day, I will raise up the tabernacle of David which has fallen down"* (NKJV). He would pause after he read that verse at the beginning of many of his messages and say to the people, "say, *that day*," and they would repeat in turn. Then he would go on to explain to them how *this day* (the one we live in now) is *that day* which was prophesied so long ago.

In other words, God is doing something in our day and time that was spoken of and prophesied about so long ago. Robert was emphatically trying to communicate that this "day of the Lord," the day he would raise up the Tabernacle of David, was not off in the distance, but it is *now* in this moment in time, waiting for us to grab hold of it and run with it.

Now you may be thinking, "this is great, but I thought this was a book about the generations working together, not worship and the Tabernacle of David." I can certainly understand that, because what most people immediately think of when they hear the phrase, "Tabernacle of David" is worship. That is thanks to awesome pioneers such as Mike Bickle and others who have unpacked this concept for the Body of Christ for many years now.

But I am including a chapter on this in this book because I feel the Tabernacle of David is about so much more than just a worship movement. It is the structure and vehicle through which the generations will rule together in this next movement of revival in the earth. The structure of the Tabernacle of David and the heart that is behind it is the "new wineskin" that will usher in a great merging and working together of the generations. This merging and working together will result in exponential apostolic impact and strength to bring about great change.

You see, the day that we live in is like no other. We live in a time in history when many of the chief prophetic signs that where spoken of in the Bible are coming to pass. Things that were prophesied and spoken more than 2000 years ago have come true in the past 75 years. One of the chief prophetic sign posts in our time is that after 2000 years of diaspora and from the ashes of the Holocaust, the nation of Israel has come back to their land. The events that Amos 9:11 describes have come true and Israel stands as a sign to all the nations that God is true to his word. His faithfulness endures to a thousand generations. The word of the Lord stands.

I believe that part of the fulfillment of the verse in Amos 9:11 has already been fulfilled in the establishment of the nation of Israel in 1948. However, part of the fulfillment has yet to come forth. If God is indeed going to raise up the Tabernacle of David in our time what does that look like? What implications does that hold? I believe that the implications are staggering and that the landscape of the Church all across the world is going to continue to change dramatically over the next fifteen to twenty years. The generations are going to lead this together.

There has been a lot of forward progress in this regard, but I personally feel that we are about to see a sudden surge of this revelation all over the world. There is a revolution coming to the current prayer movement and a fuller apostolic understanding and mobilization in the midst of it. There is a cry and call of revolution on the lips and in the hearts of millions of people who, just like that crowd on Ben Yehuda Street in Jerusalem, are ready to shake heaven and earth.

As I said, many times when people think of the Tabernacle of David, they associate it with global 24/7 worship and intercession. That is a very real part of it and the core of this movement centers around this aspect, because the core of any move of God is always the presence of God. But while some have stopped at prayer and worship meetings, God is calling us to begin to legislate the heavens and the earth from our place seated with Christ, bringing his kingdom reign onto the earth. The Tabernacle of David was not only a place of worship and intercession, but it set the culture and priority of a king and his kingdom for decades and became the seat from which God ruled and reigned over a people. God is raising this back up in our time and it is linked with apostolic centers and a people who are kingdom-minded.

An Apostolic People Who Rule

We are in a season when God is reviving ancient things and making them new again. This concept of the Tabernacle of David is over 3000 years old, yet God is breathing on it in this time. Likewise, the concept of the apostolic center or apostolic hub is millennia old, but God is releasing it afresh to his people in this time.

We need to fully understand how the Tabernacle of David is supposed to operate as well as understand the power of having an apostolic mindset. Having an apostolic mindset doesn't mean only that you have a mindset that *goes,* which is what the word implies (*apostolos* = sent one) but it also means that you have a mindset to *rule.*

The airways are highways for the trafficking of light and darkness. Many believe that angels and demons can move in dimensions that we don't yet understand and on lines that we can't see. These highways are the distribution lines for the two kingdoms. Whoever rules the air, rules the territory. As an apostolic people, we have to not only maintain, but also gain new ground in the airways over regions, territories and nations. One of the main ways that we do this is by the sound that we release.

We often find ourselves petitioning and asking when we need to be decreeing, declaring and demanding a thing. The prayer movement in America needs to shift in an apostolic direction. The people who are rising up will understand how to legislate the heavens through the sound that they release. They will say what is allowed to come into the air over a region and what is not. They will bind up powers of darkness, trying to traffic their sound and release their influence over a region and loose the hosts of heaven.

In this coming shift in the prayer movement, a power and a manifestation will be released that will turn nations. No longer will we be just a *prophetic* people who know that God is up to something and who pray and ask him to bring it forth. But we will be a people who then *move* in what has been birthed and *govern* the region to which we have been assigned. As a people, we will establish a throne for the King of Kings and the Lord of Lords, and we will do it in the sound we release.

There really is no empty space. If you look at the atmosphere of a city, wherever you go around the world, it is clear to see that something is ruling. Many times it isn't the kingdom we are looking for. Islam releases a sound five times a day that fills that space or atmosphere over a region. Wiccans releases their sound in the dead of night and at other times. The secular and political arena releases its sound all throughout the day in the news and media. But where is the sound of the Lord? It is locked behind an old pattern of asking, begging and petitioning on our knees when God is saying it is time to stand and wield our sword and take dominion.

Merging Streams

The younger David generation seems to understand the core of the "one thing" mandate. There are thousands of young people who have decided to give themselves to the house of prayer in day and night intercession. They sit at the feet of Jesus and seek his beauty in his Temple (see Psalm 27:4). They play their instruments, sing their songs and read the Word.

I was massively impacted the first time I went to the "One Thing" conference in Kansas City led by the IHOP movement. To be in a room of tens of thousands of other young people crying out and singing phrases like, "All I want is you" changed my life. I saw that I was not alone and that all over the world and even America, there is a generation of young people who want to love and serve the Lord. However, in the midst of this emphasis on intimacy with God, there seems to be a lack of an understanding of ruling, taking dominion and spiritual warfare.

The older generation seems to understand the concepts of taking dominion, faith, ruling in the place of prayer and spiritual warfare. These concepts were widely taught and understood among the older generations who experienced revival and sat under great teachers such as Derek Prince, Jack Hayford and others. But at times, activity and building great and big ministries can take precedence over sitting at the feet of Jesus and living for the "one thing."

Is one generation wrong and the other right? Or does each generation have a piece of the puzzle that the other needs and that can and will be used in this next movement? I believe that God is taking the streams and merging them in this time. He is fulfilling what he spoke through the prophet Malachi when he talked about the hearts of the generations turning toward one another. This next move of God needs each piece and cannot survive without both of them.

I believe that somehow David understood this. He understood the priority of Presence, but he also warred and took ground. Even in the psalms you can see this. One moment he speaks of the beauty of the Lord, the next he is talking about God grinding his enemies' teeth into dust! Was he schizophrenic? No. He understood that in the Tabernacle of David, there was a place for both *worship* and *war*. He understood how to establish a throne through prayer and worship.

One of the things that really concerns me when I look at the younger generation is the lack of knowledge or experience with what I would call "breakthrough prayer." What I mean by that is the down and dirty, no music, no lights, raw, pray-in-tongues type of prayer that our grandparents knew in revival.

I work with Apostle Barbara Yoder, who was connected to Myrtle D. (Mom) Beall who led a great move of God in the 1940s. Apostle Barbara tells me that if you knew how to do anything at Bethesda (the church Mom Beall led), it was pray. They knew and experienced a realm of breakthrough in prayer that unlocked miracles, signs and wonders.

Mom Beall actually had a radio program called "America to Your Knees" during World War II which was really more of a prayer meeting than a radio program. They had dozens of young men from their church go off to the war and prayed and interceded in this "breakthrough prayer" manner. Not one of those young men died in the war. They came back with accounts of miracle after miracle when God had delivered them so that he could bring them home safe.

Mom Beall saw cancers fall off people, hundreds of alcoholics delivered and set free, marriages restored and more during her ministry. She attributed much of this breakthrough and these divine interventions to the undergirding of prayer that went on in a continual way.

The younger generation needs a revelation and impartation of this "precious oil" that the Samuels have before it is gone.

Likewise, also, for the younger generation who seem more drawn to contemplative or "harp and bowl" style prayer, there is a key and strength in that too. As much as this new move needs the sword of "breakthrough prayer," it also needs the heart of love and intimacy. Sometimes we start warring when God has already won the battle.

Breaking the Mold

You see, for both generations, we need to break the mold. We tend to settle into trends and become comfortable in a particular revelation and the feeling it brings. We become echoes of the past, or of a certain leader who got a revelation for a season.

Which is more powerful, an echo in the distance or a voice speaking next to you? The voice is clear, consistent, present. It leaves a much more lasting and definite impact than an echo that you hear drifting upon the wind.

It's time to get the full strength of our voice back. One of the things that I feel is going to change in this next phase of the Tabernacle of David is that we will go from being largely *trendy*, to being truly *innovative*.

To explain fully what I mean, we have to first start by looking at the definition of the words:

101

TRENDY: A person or characteristic which is very careful to follow and emulate fashion, style or cultural influence.

So in other words, by definition, a trendy person is a person who is very smart, aware, in touch, but who *follows.* They are constantly exerting effort, time and money to keep in touch with what others are doing.

Now let's look at innovate:

INNOVATE: To create or introduce something new; to make changes to something that is established.

This word suggests a leader, a trend-setter, a creative person or organization who is constantly pushing the boundaries of what is established, normal and even possible.

I mentioned the example of an echo or a voice in the beginning of this section because it is very relevant to the Tabernacle of David movement overall. When I survey the landscape of the current movement, it looks very trendy to me in most cases. Trendy suggests an echo; it is simply riding the wave of and following behind a true, legitimate, creative voice.

We are so careful, alert, aware and smart. These are all good things, and we work so hard at it! We look at the culture, the trends, what is popular, what people are buying and reading and listening to—but in every case we are *following.* I feel this in most of the worship services that I attend, whether it is a normal Christian church service or a "house of prayer" style service.

Everyone looks the same as Bethel, Hillsong or somewhere else popular. They all sing the same songs as those places and they sound like the artists in those places. We look at places and people who are creative and innovative and try to copy and replicate that. Unfortunately, in the end we are left as an echo without much power; just a shadow, instead of setting the pace.

Now there is something to be said for looking at what others are doing well and trying to copy or replicate it. That practice is important for leaders, so I am not trying to cast a negative light on that in general, but simply to ask some questions. Could it be that what God is releasing in Bethel, although it has a large and broad impact, is the *unique* sound that God is releasing in that place? Could it be that perhaps we are missing the sights and sounds of heaven in our own church or house of prayer? Could it be that there is an explosion of creative and innovative sounds of heaven just waiting to usher forth that is unique to *you,* no matter how small or big?

A friend of mine who I greatly respect in the Body of Christ, Steve Swanson, once said to me, "I go to all these little places where revival is springing up and I hear the same songs and sounds as I do when I am at other places! I know that there is a creative sound that God wants to raise up from this place and I long to hear it! I want to hear the sound that the church in this region is making! I want to hear the cry that even the very land itself is singing and see it released on the earth!"

I feel that he is so right. Even when you look at ancient Israel and read through the songs, you can see that they were an innovative people who were led by an innovative God. They would sing songs in the season they were in. These songs would herald the season and time of God and capture the prophetic significance of whatever season that was. Their music and sound wasn't static, but rather it moved with the changing times and seasons. I often think of the way that Holy Spirit is described in the Word as a *wind.* It says in John 3:8 (NIV) that *"the wind blows wherever it pleases."* Holy Spirit is so innovative! He is constantly moving, doing and saying something new. Even the prophet Isaiah cried out, *"Behold, I will do a new thing"* (Isaiah 43:19, NKJV)!

Have you ever longed to hear what the psalms actually sounded like? I read so many times in Scripture that this or that psalm was set to stringed instruments or trumpets and I wonder, how did it sound? How did it feel as the song filled the tent of God's Presence? Did it make their hearts pound with passion in their chests? Did it make their blood boil as they felt the indignation of a righteous God burning with zeal over injustice? Did it make them want to weep in revelation of the kindness and beauty of God's compassion and mercy? Did it make them want to fall on their faces in reverent awe at his wonder, glory and majesty? Or all of the above, all at once?

I need to be honest—as a musician, I am so bored. I long for creative sounds and songs. I long for lyrics that move my heart and capture my soul. And I don't think I am the only one. I personally think that the world is starving for creativity. My heart truly breaks for some popular artists that are used and squeezed until there is no more money to be made and then cast to the side. In fact, I feel that some of them who feel lost, used and abused are going to be coming into the kingdom with this next wave of the Holy Spirit. They will be infused with the power of the Holy Spirit so they can use their gifts in the tent of God's presence. They will release songs and sounds that the world has never heard and will move in a Davidic anointing that will shape the face of a generation.

I truly believe that God wants to get us back to being innovative. When you look at the early Church in the book of Acts, you see that they were so innovative—because they had to be! More often than not, their very lives were at stake. They were not stagnant and stuck in one place, but rather they were moving and constantly advancing and creating new things and forging new paths.

This is our time to forge new paths and to have a fresh sound in our midst that is so creative and innovative that the secular world has to take notice of us and follow us instead of the other way around. We should be the most creative and innovative people on the planet!

As the generations come together in honor in the Tabernacle of David setting there will be a creative eruption. The old sounds and songs will merge with the new sounds and songs and a collaborative, beautiful symphony will spring forth. Whether you associate with the Davids or the Samuels or somewhere in between, get ready! Let go of the model you are comfortable with and embrace something new—even if it looks very old.

Look at the picture of the throne room as described in the book of Revelation:

> *And they sang a new song, saying: "You are worthy to take the scroll and to open its seals, because you were slain, and with your blood you purchased for God persons from every tribe and language and people and nation.* (Revelation 5:9, NIV)

You have all read that as many times as I have, I am sure, but consider this for a moment: Perhaps they are singing a new song because their picture and image of God shifts from moment to moment! What if he actually looks different from moment to moment? He is the same, because he is the Eternal One, but what if he reveals a new aspect of who he is in the midst of his glory moment by moment! In response, they cannot help but sing of this new revelation they have just encountered.

In God's infinite capability, anything is possible. I think we need to start asking God to let us sit in on some of those heaven sessions, to let us listen in to what is being sung and said. Wouldn't it change the status quo of our worship services if every week there was a new song that was being released that was literally dripping in heavenly revelation, hot off the press, fresh bread from heaven? These songs merge with prophetic and apostolic decrees, hearing and seeing what is happening in heaven and releasing it to shift the earth. This is where God is taking us.

There is a massive shift in understanding and practice coming to us all. We are no longer going to be, "one or the other" type of people, leaders and movements. We are coming into maturity in all things as a body and beginning to awaken again to who we are. The generations are merging together in this powerful new move and the *government of God* is beginning to issue forth from the Tabernacle of David.

There is a line in one of my favorite movies, *The Lord of the Rings*, when Gandalf, one of the main characters, is speaking of a group of beings known as the Ents. He speaks about how they have been asleep for a long time, but that they are going to, *"wake up . . . and find that they are strong."* This is our time to awaken to a functional unity together in the generations and find that we are stronger than we ever thought we were. Alone we may be defeated, but *together, we are unstoppable.*

Chapter 10

BECOMING THE BRIDGE

In Times of Crisis, the Wise Build Bridges

In the beginning of this book, I quoted a Nigerian proverb: "In the time of crisis, the wise build bridges and the foolish build dams."

This whole book is about building bridges; making points of connection, love and cooperation between the generations, even though at times we have gaping chasms between us. It is about seeing the Samuels' precious oil of wisdom, knowledge and encounter with the Holy Spirit poured onto the orphan shepherds who have a king lurking inside of them. Recently as I was praying and seeking the Lord on all of this, he encouraged me with a fresh word. He said to me, "Building bridges is good, but who is willing to become the bridge?"

I had to chew on that for a while. The meaning seemed a bit hidden from me. I began to ask the Lord to show me what he meant; what was his purpose in telling me this? I felt like he led me to begin to study bridges.

Some of the most amazing structures in the world are bridges—the structures themselves, how long they took to build, the often-immense cost involved in fabricating them. But even more impressive than the actual structure is the purpose the bridge performs.

A simple example of this is the Brooklyn Bridge in New York City. Opened to the public in 1883, it was constructed at a time when suspension bridges were just beginning to be refined and tested. There had been several horrible collapses of suspension bridges and people were a bit skeptical of them. The bridge was by far the longest of its kind at the time. In fact, some called it the "eighth wonder of the world." The bridge was built at great cost, including the cost of some dozen lives that were lost. Yet even more impressive is what it accomplished for the people of New York City.

The bridge connected Brooklyn and Manhattan for the first time, which eventually led to Brooklyn becoming a part of New York City. There were several reasons for this, but one of them was because the bridge made this important connection. Because Manhattan is an island, the only way those from Brooklyn or Manhattan (a financial and cultural center) could reach one another was by ferry. The bridge gave people a way to walk, bicycle, ride on horseback or by horse-drawn carriage. (Other road vehicles hadn't yet been commercially developed.) The commerce which emerged because of the bridge was phenomenal.

This is just one of many examples. When a bridge is built, the implications of its creation go far beyond just the assembly and functionality of the structure itself. It creates passage, connects regions and people, saves time, bolsters economy, makes travel safer and so much more.

So where am I going with this? In trying to understand what the Lord was showing me, I began to see a bit of what he meant when he asked me the question, "who will become the bridge?" When we look at the rivers, gorges and chasms between the generations that need to be connected, it is easy to build strategy and implement plans to connect the dots. If you are the foreman or the designer, you can basically stay out of the construction process. You don't pound the rivets into the cold, hard iron. You don't walk the very dangerous metal beams as the wind tries to blow you off. Only those which are working know those experiences. Or even deeper than the worker, what about the very material itself? I know I'm reaching here, but try to imagine with me.

The iron is forged in extreme temperatures of heat, bent and forced into the perfect position. Then it is transported to the place of use, where it is hammered and laid into its place along with all the other pieces. And then . . . it stays. It doesn't move. Through the scorching summer heat and the bitter cold winter as the wind whips all around, it remains still, solid and in place. It never will let go of the steel that it is connected to, nor force out the rivets that are driven deep into it. It knows its purpose and does not waver. In a sense, it is given over fully to the Master's hand and will. It is used strategically for a life of sacrifice as it stays in position and lets all others use it and walk all over it.

What if all the iron of the Brooklyn Bridge suddenly decided that it had a mind of its own and knew better than the master creator? After-all, it was put in place over 130 years ago. What if it decided it was tired of the scorching heat or the long, cold winters? It is far too hard to live this life of sacrifice. What if one day, the iron components of the bridge start to speak and they form a union and then they get up and leave all at once? They form a plan to get up, disconnect from each other, force out the rivets and plunge into the river below. Quite a tragedy would ensue. Cars and people would be lost by the hundreds. The connection, accessibility and more would be lost and broken.

I know these are elemental examples, but the point I feel the Lord was trying to make to me is clear. If bridges are to be created and formed, they require *material.* I believe that you and I are the material he is looking for. He is not so much looking for us to *form connections*, but rather to lay our lives down in humility and *become the connections,* even as the iron is laid into place on a bridge.

Where are those in both generations who are willing to become the bridge, to be put in place as pieces of iron, immovable and unshakable, willing to sacrifice? Where are those who are reaching out a hand to others to form a bond that will stretch across the divide? It is not an easy task, but one that must be done. This bond *must be formed.* I feel it is far more important than we may realize. It can't just be one generation. It has to be both the older and the younger. The Samuels have to arise and go, and the Davids have to receive the oil and then endure through the tests and trials which will soon follow.

This is one of the verses in Scripture which had always rocked my world and moved me deeply:

And he will turn the hearts of the fathers to the children, and the hearts of the children to their fathers, lest I come and strike the earth with a curse. (Malachi 4:6, NKJV)

This verse declares the necessity for *both hearts* to turn. Briefly, I want to look at a few keys for both generations as they turn and become the answer to the prayers they are praying.

A Time for Action

I love concepts. One of my favorite places to live is in the realm of concepts ideas, dreams and what may be possible. I love to ponder on the best-case scenario for things, the potential of people, organizations and movements. But truth be told, if concepts don't turn into actions, then all we have are pipe dreams, empty intentions and hope deferred.

Richie Norton has been featured in *Forbes, Entrepreneur, Bloomberg Businessweek* and other publications that are highly respected. He says, "Action is the bridge between thought and reality."

A lot of what I have laid out in this book is thought. You may or may not think it is great thought; regardless, turning those thoughts into reality requires action.

I have many Jewish friends. There is a word in modern Hebrew: *tachlis.* It has a funny meaning—it basically means, "brass tacks." In other words, you stop talking in theory, generalities and concepts and you get down to the practical details of a matter.

Enough talking. Enough dreaming. Now is the time. A movement of God is coming forth now. A generational revolution happening and action is required of us all.

I want ask you: What action are you feeling led to take after reading the previous nine chapters? Whom do you need to call on the phone, email, text or take to coffee? Whom do you need to forgive, reconcile with or let back into your heart? What perspectives and assumptions do you need to change about the other generation, whether you are a Samuel or a David? Think and pray through it carefully and allow the Holy Spirit to guide you.

Then—*tachlis!* Take action.

Use Your Material Wisely

They say that beauty is in the eye of the beholder, and I believe that is true. Another truism might be that the ultimate potential of something is in the hands of the one who holds it. A piece of wood in my hands would probably be good for only a few things, most of them destructive. To be honest, I love to make fires, and that's probably what I would use a piece of wood for. But a master craftsman like my father would fix something, create something or carve something. The same material that can be used for waste and destruction can likewise be used for something very good and creative. It's all up to the decisions of the one who holds the material.

The late Joseph Fort Newton, the author of *Everyday Religion*, repeated this line: "Men build too many walls and not enough bridges."

You are building material, like iron, in God's hand. The same material that can be used to build an amazing bridge can also be used to fortify a wall of division. It is clear which purpose for which God desires to use the material of your life, energy and passion, but the choice is yours.

In 1 Corinthians 3 the Bible compares us in a very unique way to a house that God is building. The description is preceded by this exhortation at the beginning of the chapter:

And I, brethren, could not speak to you as to spiritual people but as to carnal, as to babes in Christ. I fed you with milk and not with solid food; for until now you were not able to receive it, and even now you are still not able; for you are still carnal. For where there are envy, strife, and divisions among you, are you not carnal and behaving like mere men? For when one says, "I am of Paul," and another, "I am of Apollos," are you not carnal? (1 Corinthians 3: 1–4, NKJV)

I can hear the echoes of the declarations, "I am of Paul! I am of Apollos!" as they come into the here and now. It sounds like, "I am a Millennial! I am a Generation X! I am a Baby Boomer!" and so on. We affiliate with a certain label because we think it is somehow important to our identity. There is redemptive identity in every generation, but all of that is overshadowed in Christ. Paul told the Corinthians to stop perpetuating these divisions. He said, "Stop acting like mere men. You have been called to be the representation of Jesus Christ in the earth, not ordinary, carnal-minded people!"

It's true to the present day. Remember, become the bridge! An amazing thing about a bridge is that it is not one-sided. It is connected to both sides equally. It has a vested interest in both sides. It knows that its success as a bridge is tied to both sides equally. Should one side fall or fail, *all is lost.*

We need each other! We can use the material of our life to build *with* and *for* the Lord and each other—or *against,* as Paul goes on to say:

For we are God's fellow workers; you are God's field, you are God's building. According to the grace of God which was given to me, as a wise master builder I have laid the foundation, and another builds on it. But let each one take heed how he builds on it. (1 Corinthians 3: 9–10, NKJV)

We are God's *fellow workers.* We are supposed to work *with* him. If he desires the iron of our lives to be used to build a bridge and we get up and instead try to insert ourselves securely into a wall, we are not fulfilling our purpose in working with him.

I am a father and I love my kids. Recently, I was painting the walls for my wife's birthday. My kids love to be with me and do everything that I am doing. They are three and four years old and want desperately to be thirty-five. Every adult thing that I do is automatically something that they want to do. So, when I was painting and spackling and sanding, they wanted to do it as well.

Now, red was one of the colors my wife wanted me to use. I knew that if I let them even attempt to help me with the painting of these walls, that this red color would be all over them, me, the carpet, the dog, the neighbors, their hair... you get the picture. Even though they wanted to help me, they didn't have the skill or the wisdom.

Sometimes in our journey, in trying to serve the Lord and partner with him, we do the same thing. We want to take the red paint of our passion and gloriously spread it everywhere! But that isn't the same as working with the Lord as a fellow worker; it's more like working against him. In these bridges that are being constructed, the Master knows best. He knows where to put the iron of your life. It is best to yield to him and let him position you. Don't work on your own. In your best intentions you might be helping to create a wall instead of a bridge.

If we are going to achieve the type of unity and understanding we are talking about—to create a culture of honor that unites us all—we need to be bridge people, those who are able to lie down and sacrifice so that both sides can be connected to one another and therefore become useful. There are many who have gone before us, and I believe their message to us, almost like a whisper coming from the cloud of witnesses, is this: Lay your life down in sacrifice without asking anything in return. Let the Lord securely fasten you into this grand structure he is creating.

The heroes of movements are not always those who are in the public eye. It is those who sacrifice behind closed doors where no one sees who make all the difference. The hero of the bridge is the iron that endures all the different seasons of the environment where it has been secured into place.

God has called us to selflessness and servanthood. Instead of trying to win over the other generation to our side, what if we instead reached out a hand?

Imagine two pieces of rope at opposite ends of a gorge. Both ropes want the other to come to them first; therefore, neither ever moves. Neither rope ever fulfills its destiny. They remain as singular entities instead of turning to one another, stretching out in love and openness of heart and making a connection that gives them both the fulfillment of their destiny—to become one. In becoming one, they provide a service to others, which could otherwise never happen, a way across the gorge.

It all has to start somewhere, with someone. You who are reading this—is it you?

A Legacy of Hope

> *For the LORD will not forsake His people, for His great name's sake, because it has pleased the LORD to make you His people. Moreover, as for me, far be it from me that I should sin against the LORD in ceasing to pray for you; but I will teach you the good and the right way. Only fear the LORD, and serve Him in truth with all your heart; for consider what great things He has done for you.* (1 Samuel 12:22–24, NKJV)

I love the Lord. He never leaves us without hope. In the midst of all of the struggles and challenges that seem as chasms for us to cross, there is always a promise of redemption. The Scripture verse above records some of the last words of Samuel the prophet. He chastens the people of Israel when they come to him and he warns them sternly, but in the end, leaves them with a reminder of God's faithfulness.

God is faithful to visit every generation. He moves by his Spirit in the midst of impossible odds and circumstances and shows each generation that he is who he says he is. I know that even in the midst of the challenges we face, God will come. There will be men and women of iron in each generation who will lay their lives down to create a bridge of righteousness for generations to come. That pathway will lead us into a new place where we have never been before. It will create a miracle highway, suspended high above the raging waters of this world.

The power that will be unlocked from the synergy of the generations will form a prototype. Many others can walk in those footsteps. It will lead us to an outpouring of God's glory upon the earth like nothing we have ever seen or heard of before. This is our inheritance, our manifest destiny.

A new breed of Samuels and Davids is arising in the earth. *Now* is the time and *you* are the people!

ABOUT THE AUTHOR

Benjamin A. Deitrick has been in full time ministry since the age of 17. For the first 10 years of his ministry, he resided in New York and served alongside Eagles Wings Ministries under the direction of Bishop Robert Stearns. During this time, he was involved in conference and itinerant ministry in a variety of capacities including speaking, leading worship and being a part of prayer ministry teams. In 2011, Benjamin and his wife Tarrah felt the call to move to Ann Arbor, MI. and to serve Shekinah Regional Apostolic Center under the leadership of Apostle Barbara J. Yoder.

Last year, Apostle Barbara Yoder handed over the reigns of leading the local church to Pastors Benjamin and Tarrah Deitrick. Benjamin now presides as the Lead Pastor of Shekinah. Over the last 16 years of full-time ministry, Benjamin has had the opportunity to travel to 22 of the 50 United States and 23 nations ministering and preaching the word of God with demonstrations of power. Benjamin is married to the love of his life, has two small children and currently resides in Ann Arbor, MI. His desire is to see an apostolic and prophetic people engulfed in the flames of revival, rise as an army in the earth to fulfill the mandate of the great commission.

RESOURCES

For more information about Benjamin Deitrick, to coordinate him to speak at your church or event, or for more information on Shekinah Regional Apostolic Center in Ann Arbor, please write, call or visit our website:

Shekinah Regional Apostolic Center
P. O. Box 2485
4600 Scio Church rd.
Ann Arbor, MI. 48103

info@shekinahchurch.org

Telephone: (734) 662-6040
Fax: (734) 662-5470

www.shekinahchurch.org

OTHER RESOURCES FROM THE AUTHOR

Building the Future Together: Functional Unity Among the Generations by: Benjamin Deitrick

Available for sale in CD and DVD format at:
www.shekinahchurch.org

Fourth Man in the Fire: Celebrating Victory in the Midst of Trial by: Benjamin Deitrick

Available for sale in CD and DVD format at:
www.shekinahchurch.org

The Dominion Mandate: Recovering the Glory by: Benjamin Deitrick

Available for sale in CD and DVD format at:
www.shekinahchurch.org